D0845924

J. A. Schwarz

PSYCHODYNAMIC PSYCHOTHERAPY OF BORDERLINE PATIENTS

PSYCHODYNAMIC PSYCHOTHERAPY OF BORDERLINE PATIENTS

OTTO F. KERNBERG, M.D.

MICHAEL A. SELZER, M.D.

HAROLD W. KOENIGSBERG, M.D.

ARTHUR C. CARR, Ph.D.

ANN H. APPELBAUM, M.D.

Basic Books, Inc., Publishers   *New York*

Selections from chapter 3 are reprinted from Michael A. Selzer, Harold W. Koenigsberg, and Otto F. Kernberg, "The Initial Contract in the Treatment of Borderline Patients," *American Journal of Psychiatry* 144 (1987): 927–30. Copyright © 1987 The American Psychiatric Association. Reprinted by permission.

Selections from chapter 6 are reprinted from Otto F. Kernberg, "Projection and Projective Identification: Developmental and Clinical Aspects," *Journal of the American Psychoanalytic Association* 35 (1987): 795–819. Copyright © 1987 International Universities Press. Reprinted by permission.

Library of Congress Cataloging-in-Publication Data

Psychodynamic psychotherapy of borderline patients
Otto F. Kernberg et al.

   Bibliography: p. 199
   Includes Index.
   ISBN 0–465–06643–7
   1. Borderline personality disorder—Treatment. 2. Psychotherapy.
I. Kernberg, Otto F., 1928–
RC569.5.B67P79 1989   89–6738
616.85′852—dc20   CIP

Copyright © 1989 by Otto F. Kernberg, Michael A. Selzer,
Harold W. Koenigsberg, Arthur C. Carr, and Ann H. Appelbaum
Printed in the United States of America
Designed by Vincent Torre
89 90 91 92 HC 9 8 7 6 5 4 3 2 1

CONTENTS

PART THREE
COMMON COMPLICATIONS

PREFACE

———————

This book presents recommendations on the conduct of a psychotherapy tailored for borderline patients. It developed out of the requirements of a psychotherapy research program at The New York Hospital–Cornell Medical Center, Westchester Division.

Recently, the state of the art in psychotherapy research has placed special emphasis upon a rigorous specification of the treatment under study. Detailed descriptions of treatments are necessary to identify key therapeutic ingredients, to indicate how various treatments are distinct from each other, to permit uniform training of therapists, and to verify that a treatment is delivered to the patient in its intended form. To these ends, the present handbook was developed. The authors hope that a detailed and operational description of a therapy for borderline patients will also serve as a resource for practitioners.

The presentation of a psychotherapy in handbook format is inherently problematic. Psychotherapy is a process whose very direction from moment to moment depends upon the sum total of all that has already transpired. The data upon which the therapist bases decisions come not only from the patient's speech content, but also from subjective perceptions of the patient as well as the therapist's own introspections. Just as the patient's thoughts and behaviors are multiply determined, so too is the therapist's intervention at each moment. There are many equally valid pathways to therapeutic progress.

Our book is not intended by itself to teach how to carry out psychodynamic psychotherapy with borderline patients. The conduct of psychotherapy is a complex skill that is achieved only through the combination of didactic teaching, closely supervised clinical practice, and the development of the student's own capacity for introspection. This book can be an adjunct to that process for the beginning therapist and a handbook for the more experienced. It is written for clinicians who are familiar with the psychodynamic model and who have had experience in the conduct of psychoanalytically oriented psychotherapy. Familiarity in working with transference and countertransference issues is assumed.

The reader of a psychotherapy handbook must beware of many pitfalls. Handbooks tend to be reductionistic. By implication, they posit a standard sequence of maneuvers to be carried out. In placing emphasis upon technique, they often downplay the role of the interpersonal context of the treatment. Sometimes they suggest that there is one correct approach. Often they do not do justice to the human diversity of patients.

We have tried to resist such simplifying distortions in developing this handbook, yet a codification of a therapy can create the illusion that what is not incorporated is irrelevant. We want to emphasize that this book is an outline of what we believe to be necessary and sufficient constituents of the treatment, not an attempt to be all-inclusive. We ask the reader to remain open to the complexities and nuances that cannot be contained in a book intended to present guidelines for the conduct of therapy; prescribed interventions may have to be delayed or modified because of circumstances of the moment. Sequences may not always be followed in order; sometimes a few steps are carried out and the loop is repeated before moving on.

The treatment model presented in this handbook reflects an approach to the psychotherapy of borderline patients based upon an ego psychology–object relations conceptualization. Both the treatment strategy and the tactics derive from an integrated theoretical model of borderline psychopathology. In spite of the varying conceptions of the term *borderline,* a surprising degree of agreement has developed about the treatment of choice for these patients, namely, a psychoanalytically oriented psychotherapy that relies on transference interpretation. Ranging from the Kleinian therapy of Herbert Rosenfeld; an ego psychology orientation as described by such writers as John Frosch and Ralph Greenson; an American object relations approach as represented by Mardi J. Horowitz, Edith Jacobson, Otto F. Kernberg, and Margaret S. Mahler; and the British middle group represented by Donald Winnicott and Margaret Little; to ego psychologists of this country interested in the object relations approach, including Peter Giovac-chini, James Masterson, Donald Rinsley, and Gerald Adler, writers from quite different theoretical perspectives have arrived at strikingly similar approaches to treatment. The groups influenced by Heinz Kohut and the New York Psychoanalytic Institute study group led by Sander Abend, Michael Porder, and Martin Willick may be exceptions to this generalization, although both groups have generally reported experience with patients who are healthier than the ordinary borderline patient. This handbook operationalizes the treatment approach described by Kernberg and derived from ego psychology–object relations theory.

Many have contributed to the development of this book. The authors are all members of the Borderline Psychotherapy Research Project led by John Clarkin and Harold Koenigsberg at The New York Hospital–Cornell Medical Center, Westchester Division. They drew upon ideas from the entire membership of this research group, including Stephen Bauer, Paulina Kernberg, Lawrence Rockland, and Frank Yeomans. We are grateful also to the research therapists who participated in the treatment of our patients.

Our research assistants, Marion Zaretzky and Maria Gomez-Vecslir, made the data collection and the conduct of the research treatments possible. In the development of this book, we have benefited from the advice and suggestions of Arnold Cooper, William Frosch, John G. Gunderson, Mardi J. Horowitz, Gerald L. Klerman, Marsha Linehan, Lester Luborsky, Robert Michels, Nancy Miller, Ernst Ticho, and Robert Wallerstein. Responsibility for this book's shortcomings, however, rests with the authors. Above all, we thank the patients who participated in our research study, choosing to endure the unique hardships of being a patient in a psychotherapy research project, because of their interest in adding to an understanding of the therapeutic process. Our patients over the years have been teachers to us, and all have played a role in enriching this book.

PART ONE

PRINCIPLES OF TREATMENT

CHAPTER 1

Borderline Pathology and Psychotherapeutic Alternatives

Borderline Pathology

During the 1950s, psychotherapists and psychoanalysts began to describe a group of patients who could consciously experience primary process material but who lacked the capacity for introspection, insight, and working through (Kernberg, 1980). They often showed severe mood swings as well as a striking tendency to perceive significant others as all good or all bad. Negating the traditional conceptualization of libidinal stages, these patients showed strong oral trends, but simultaneously presented strong aggressive tendencies that related to all levels of psychosexual development, especially to their oedipal strivings. In short, these patients defied all efforts to hypothesize the origin of their difficulties by situating the particular point of libidinal development.

Because these patients were puzzling from the standpoint of psychoanalytic models then prevailing, the earliest conceptualization of the term *borderline* was a very broad one, somewhat synonymous with "the difficult patient." Although they presumably showed generally good reality-testing ability, these patients nevertheless might suddenly experience severe transference regressions that belied their "neurotic" status. Dynamically, they showed a condensation of oedipal and preoedipal conflicts whose psychogenic origins were postulated to reside in the rapprochement subphase of the stage of separation-individuation (Mahler, 1972, 1979; Mahler, Pine, & Bergman, 1975). *Borderline* has sometimes continued to be used in this broad and somewhat vague sense. The term caught favor because of its relation to the common language of psychotherapists, but lacks diagnostic precision and thus is of little value for purposes of research.

Efforts to achieve uniformity in the characterization of these difficult patients have led to more precise approaches to the definition of the term *borderline.* Perhaps the most narrow approach is represented by the concept "borderline personality disorder" as defined by the American Psychiatric Association in its *Diagnostic and Statistical Manual of Mental Disorders* (DSMIII) in 1980 and in its later revision (DSMIII-R) in 1987. These definitions are based upon descriptive, circumscribed, and phenomenologic features. The DSMIII-R criteria for borderline personality disorder are that the individual's long-term functioning should be characterized by at least *five* of the following (1987, p. 347):

1. a pattern of unstable and intense interpersonal relationships characterized by alternating between extremes of overidealization and devaluation
2. impulsiveness in at least two areas that are potentially self-damaging, e.g., spending, sex, substance use, shoplifting, reckless driving, binge eating (Do not include suicidal or self-mutilating behavior covered in [5].)
3. affective instability: marked shifts from baseline mood to depression, irritability, or anxiety, usually lasting a few hours and only rarely more than a few days
4. inappropriate, intense anger or lack of control of anger, e.g., frequent displays of temper, constant anger, recurrent physical fights
5. recurrent suicidal threats, gestures, or behavior, or self-mutilating behavior
6. marked and persistent identity disturbance manifested by uncertainty about at least two of the following: self-image, sexual

orientation, long-term goals or career choice, type of friends desired, preferred values

7. chronic feelings of emptiness or boredom
8. frantic efforts to avoid real or imagined abandonment (Do not include suicidal or self-mutilating behavior covered in [5].)

Although suited for research purposes, this approach to diagnosis—which was derived in large part from the work of John G. Gunderson and Jonathan E. Kolb (1978), Christopher J. Perry and Gerald L. Klerman (1980), and Theodore Millon (1981)—has proved less than ideal for clinical purposes because it fails to distinguish the common features of severe personality disorders from those of the less severe ones. Furthermore, because the DSMIII-R criteria overlap those of other severe personality disorders (particularly the schizotypal, histrionic, antisocial, and narcissistic), the designation has carried too little implication for or relation to etiology, treatment, or prognosis (Kernberg, 1984).

Perhaps less precise but bearing more relevance to a presumed etiology of the disorder, as well as to the treatment considered best for its resolution, has been the concept of *borderline personality organization,* which is not only descriptive but structural. As elucidated by Kernberg, the diagnosis of borderline personality organization is based on three structural criteria: identity diffusion, level of defensive operations, and capacity for reality testing.

IDENTITY DIFFUSION

Identity diffusion is defined as the lack of integration of the concept of the self or significant others. It is revealed in patients' subjective experience of chronic emptiness, contradictory self-perceptions, contradictory behavior, impoverished and contradictory perceptions of others, and inability to convey themselves and their significant interactions with others to an interviewer—who as a consequence experiences difficulty in empathizing with them and their significant others. The assumptions underlying this lack of integration are discussed elsewhere (Kernberg, 1975).

LEVEL OF DEFENSIVE OPERATIONS

In contrast to neurotic personality organization, in which the patient's defensive organization centers on repression and other advanced or high-level defensive operations, borderline and psychotic levels of organization manifest predominantly primitive defenses centering on the mechanism of splitting. Splitting and other mechanisms related to it (for example, primitive idealization, projective identification, denial, omnipotent control, and devaluation) protect the ego from conflict by dissociating contradictory experiences of the self and of significant others.

The presence of splitting and its related primitive defense mechanisms may be elicited in the analysis of the patient's personality, as reflected in interactions both with significant others and with an interviewer.

Splitting. The division of self and external objects into "all good" and "all bad" results in sudden and complete reversals of all feelings and conceptualizations about one's self or views about a particular person.

Primitive Idealization. This mechanism exaggerates the tendency to see external objects as good. The qualities of goodness in others are exaggerated in a pathological way, to the exclusion of commonplace human defects. The patient does not tolerate any imperfection in the idealized person. The counterpart of idealization is the complete devaluation of others, or the perception of others as persecutory and dangerous.

Early Forms of Projection; Projective Identification. In contrast to higher levels of projection, characterized by attributing to other persons an impulse that the patient has repressed, projective identification is characterized by: (1) the tendency to continue to experience the impulse, which is at the same time projected onto the other person; (2) fear of the other person, who is viewed as being characterized by or under the sway of that projected impulse; and (3) the need to control that person, often done in such a way as to elicit behavior in the person that seemingly validates the projection. Thus, whereas projection is based on an ego structure centered on repression as a defense, projective identification is based on a structure centered on splitting, or primitive dissociation (Kernberg 1987).

Denial. In borderline patients denial is exemplified by the presence of emotionally independent areas of consciousness. These patients are aware that their perceptions, thoughts, and feelings about themselves or others at some times are completely opposite those entertained at other times, but this recognition has no emotional relevance and cannot influence their current state of mind.

Omnipotence and Devaluation. Both omnipotence and devaluation are derivatives of splitting and are represented by the activation of ego states that reflect a highly inflated grandiose, omnipotent self and that relate to depreciated and devaluated representations of others, including the projection of devalued aspects of the self. Further elaborations of all these primitive defensive operations and clinical illustrations of them are presented in chapter 6.

CAPACITY FOR REALITY TESTING

In both neurotic and borderline personality organizations, the capacity for reality testing is retained, but this is not the case at a psychotic level of personality organization. Reality testing is defined as the capacity to differentiate self from nonself and intrapsychic from external origins of perceptions and stimuli, and to evaluate one's own affect, behavior, and thought content in terms of ordinary social norms. Loss of this capacity must be differentiated from alterations in the *subjective experience of reality* (things feel strange but the patient is fully aware of reality) that may be present in any patient with psychological distress, and from the alteration of the *relation to reality* (behavior is inappropriate but reality is perfectly evaluated) that is present in all character pathology, as well as in more regressed, psychotic conditions (Frosch, 1964).

Borderline personality organization also shows itself in secondary structural characteristics, such as nonspecific manifestations of ego weakness (lack of impulse control, lack of anxiety tolerance, and lack of developed channels for sublimation), superego pathology (infantile or immature value systems, contradictary internal moral demands, or even antisocial features), and in the chronic and chaotic object relations that are a direct consequence of identity diffusion and prevailing primitive defensive operations. Although these secondary structural characteristics relate to the severity of the disorder and affect its prognosis, they are not related to its diagnosis, which depends on the criteria of identity diffusion, defensive operations, and reality testing.

Purpose of the Book

In what follows, the authors have attempted to spell out the psychotherapy they regard as most suitable for patients showing characteristics of borderline personality organization. As such, this designation includes a larger group of patients than the DSMIII-R category of borderline personality disorder, and covers a level of character pathology that includes most cases of infantile or histrionic and narcissistic personalities, practically all schizoid, paranoid, "as if," and hypomanic* personalities and *all* antisocial personalities.†

As conceptualized, this treatment (which we call expressive psychotherapy or expressive therapy) is based on a psychodynamic model. For this reason, its application requires therapists who are knowledgeable about transference phenomena, defense mechanisms, resistances, and interpretive techniques. Although this particular therapy calls for some modifications in the therapist's usual technique, particularly regarding transference management and issues of technical neutrality, it follows generally accepted principles of psychoanalytic treatment. The nonspecific aspects of all psychotherapy (continuity, acceptance, reliability, genuineness, and so on) are assumed to operate here, too.

Overall Treatment Aims and Methods

Expressive psychotherapy for borderline psychopathology is designed to enhance the borderline patient's ability to experience self and others as coherent, integrated, realistically perceived individuals, and to reduce the need to use defenses that weaken ego structure by reducing the repertoire of available responses. As a result, the patient may be expected to develop an increased capacity to control impulses, tolerate anxiety, modulate affect, sublimate instinctual needs, develop stable and satisfying interpersonal relationships, and experience intimacy and love.

These aims are accomplished through the diagnosis and clarification of the dissociated or split-off components of the patient's internal

---

*"As if" and hypomanic categories are not included in DSMIII-R.

†The proposed psychotherapy is contraindicated for most patients with an antisocial personality disorder.

object world as they are revealed in rapidly emerging transferences to the therapist. These components of every transference disposition always include a self representation, an object representation, and an affective disposition that links them. The transference that develops is primitive, reflecting the patient's efforts to avoid conflict by unrealistically cleaving the loving and hating aspects of both self and others into separate parts such that even when they appear together in consciousness, they do so without influencing each other. The recommended therapy for borderline patients is the consistent approach to understanding and interpreting the transference. Rather than gratifying the patient's present needs or demands by more supportive techniques, a frequent temptation for the therapist, this therapy attempts to integrate by means of interpretation the dissociated aspects of the patient's psychic experience.

Through the process of continuously clarifying and interpreting these dissociated elements, part self representations become gradually integrated into a total self representation that includes aggressive and libidinal tendencies; by the same token, part object representations become integrated into total object representations that again combine the aggressive with the libidinal. The end result is a more differentiated and accurate view of the self and the object world, and an evolving differentiated sense of internal affect dispositions. The integrated object representations will then reflect more realistic parental images and interactions with them as perceived in early childhood. Only at this point can the borderline patient be helped to come to terms with the past more realistically, in the context of profound transformations of the current relationship to the therapist and to significant others.

The central treatment goal of integrating part self and object representations is based on the assumption that dissociated internalized object relations acquire their primitive absolute nature precisely by virtue of the dissociative act that completely separates aggression from love, creating either totally idealized or totally persecutory relations between the self and others. Integration is facilitated by the analysis of the defensive operations that actively maintain these split-off states. A central technique with these patients includes diagnosis and interpretive integration of primitive dissociated ego states in the context of the interpretive resolution of the defensive operations that maintain them as separate and split off from each other.

Contrast with Other Techniques

The basic techniques of expressive psychotherapy are the same as those of psychoanalysis: interpretation, transference analysis, and technical neutrality. These techniques are used differently, however, in the treatment of borderline disorders (see table 1.1). To begin with, this psychotherapy is carried out in a face-to-face position, and the instructions for open and continuous communication of what is on the patient's mind reflect a modification of the standard rule of free association. Also, sessions usually take place two or three times a week.

In contrast to psychoanalysis, expressive psychotherapy with borderline patients emphasizes the "here-and-now" during the major part of the treatment. Only in advanced stages of the treatment are "there-and-then" interpretations introduced; psychoanalysis proper introduces *genetic* interpretations, linking past to present behavior, at a much earlier stage in the treatment.

Again, in contrast to psychoanalysis, analysis of the transference with borderline patients is consistently modified by considering any transference interpretation in the context of what is going on in the patient's present life, in order to avoid the danger that treatment and transference interpretation themselves will be so gratifying as to impede the overcoming of the patient's difficulties. Otherwise, the therapy may become isolated from the rest of the patient's life, and used in a dissociative fashion to avoid the pain of everyday living.

Another distinction from psychoanalysis is that the severity of the borderline patient's acting out often forces the therapist out of the position of technical neutrality, which has to be reinstated interpretively as soon as the threat to the treatment that necessitated the parameter is no longer present.

In contrast to supportive treatment, expressive psychotherapy tries to maintain technical neutrality whenever possible. In supportive therapy, praise, encouragement, persuasion, advice giving, and environmental intervention may be used freely. Such supportive interventions are avoided in the expressive psychotherapy of borderline patients. When supportive work is needed, it is carried out by auxiliary therapists, if possible. In supportive treatment there is usually no analysis of transference, though there may be confrontation and reeducative reduction of the transference by pointing out its inappropriate nature. In

TABLE 1.1

Treatment Contrasts

		Psychoanalysis	Expressive Psychotherapy	Supportive Psychotherapy
Interpretive Process	Clarification Confrontation.	Prerequisites to interpretation.	Prerequisites to interpretation.	Major strategies.
	Interpretation per se [Here-and-now There-and-then]	Major strategy.	Major strategy. Only in later stages.	Replaced by cognitive and affective support and environmental intervention.
Transference Analysis		Major treatment goal.	Major treatment goal but external reality and long-term therapy goals must always be monitored.	Managed rather than analyzed. Reduced through clarification, emphasis upon the reality of the relationship, and/or displaced onto extra-transferential objects.
Technical Neutrality		Maintained throughout.	Maintained when possible. May be lost at times by patient acting out. Then to be reinstituted with interpretive technique.	Freely sacrificed and not necessarily reinstated.

summary, supportive psychotherapy uses clarification and confrontation, but not interpretation, while expressive psychotherapy avoids direct expression of affective and cognitive support, as well as environmental intervention.

In what follows, the expressive psychotherapy for borderline patients is presented as a handbook. This is geared to therapists who have a general knowledge of psychoanalytic psychotherapies and some experience in carrying out such treatment, or who will have the opportunity to carry out this specific type of psychotherapy for borderline patients under supervision. Senior therapists and psychoanalysts should be able to apply the proposed guidelines directly and independently in their practice. Junior and beginning psychotherapists should have the opportunity to discuss the proposed techniques with more senior and experienced colleagues. It is to be understood that a guide for doing psychotherapy should never supersede good clinical judgment; it is to inform and advise, rather than to mandate.

CHAPTER 2

The Treatment Approach

The theory that underlies the proposed expressive psychotherapy for borderline patients is based on a conception of a stable, pathological intrapsychic structure that determines both the major behavioral characteristics of borderline conditions and the psychotherapeutic techniques geared to deal with them. According to general psychoanalytic theory, the structural organization of classical psychoneuroses and neurotic characters is based upon a well-differentiated tripartite psychic system (that is, a well-differentiated ego, superego, and id, which are involved in intersystemic conflicts); neuroses are expressed in impulse-defense configurations that reflect unconscious intrapsychic conflicts.

The theory of borderline personality organization proposes an early pathological intrapsychic organization of borderline patients that differs from neurotic personality organization in two ways: first, in the nature of the intrapsychic conflicts that are at the basis of the pathological organization; and second, more important, in the structural conditions within which these conflicts are expressed. The dominant conflictual constellation of neurotic personality organization is the oedipus complex, which reflects the culmination of the development of sexual and aggressive drives in the context of the representational world of early childhood. In contrast, borderline personality organization shows a predominance of preoedipal conflicts and their psychic representations condensed with representations of the oedipal phase. This means that the typical triangular sexual conflicts (the themes of seduction, castration anxiety, and the primal scene) are infiltrated with themes derived from the earliest relationship between the child and the mother, aggressive drive derivatives expressing oral and anal conflicts, and, above all, a fantastic distortion of triangular relations by superimposed primitive, aggression-tinged preoedipal ones.

More important in conceptualizing a treatment model, however, is the characteristic structure of borderline personality organization. Here, intrapsychic conflicts are not predominantly repressed and therefore unconsciously dynamic; rather they are expressed in mutually dissociated ego states that reflect the defense of primitive dissociation, or splitting. These mutually dissociated ego states reflect, in fact, a primitive ego-id matrix that predates the differentiation of ego from id by means of a repressive barrier. This primitive ego-id matrix coincides with the primitive dissociation and projection of superego precursors in the form of paranoid dispositions, unconscious enactment of sadistic superego precursors, and a desperate search for idealized superego precursors. What happens in these cases is that generalized primitive dissociative or splitting mechanisms segregate contradictory aspects of early object relations within the defensively dissociated ego-id matrix, and within the defensively dissociated and partially projected superego precursors as well. In short, intrapsychic conflicts are expressed in the activation of primitive internalized object relations that predate the consolidation of the definite ego, superego, and id. These relations manifest themselves directly in the transference as apparently chaotic states that, upon psychotherapeutic exploration, reveal themselves to be constituted typically by the combination of a primitive self representation, a primitive object representation, and a primitive affect state linking them.

Contemporary psychoanalytic theory assumes that this pathological structuring of intrapsychic conflict within a primitive psychic matrix derives from a fixation at or regression to an early stage of development that predates object constancy and the consolidation of the tripartite structure, coinciding with the stage of development that Margaret Mahler (1972) described as separation-individuation. During this early stage of development, which occupies roughly the second through fourth years of life, severely pathological relationships with a parental object (whether constitutionally determined, psychologically motivated, or environmentally stimulated by severe aggression in early psycho-

14

logical experiences) determine a fixation at a level of development that is insufficiently integrated. The psychic organization becomes defensively fixated at this poorly integrated stage.

The general theory of psychotherapeutic techniques derived from this formulation focuses on the activation of primitive internalized object relations that are manifest in the transference as apparently chaotic affect states. These first have to be diagnosed and then gradually interpretively transformed from split-off or "part" object relations into integrated or "total" object relations, from primitive transferences into the advanced transferences of normal oedipal development.

A central concern in this psychotherapeutic approach is the analysis of the transference, which consists of the analysis of the reactivation in the here-and-now of past internalized object relations and also constitutes the analysis of the building blocks of ego, superego, and id. These transferences reflect internalized object relations, but not necessarily the actual object relations from the patient's past. Rather, they reflect a combination of realistic and fantasied—and often highly distorted—internalizations of such past object relations and defenses against them under the effects of activation and projection of instinctual drive derivatives. The major task in the psychotherapy of borderline patients is to bring the unconscious transference meanings in the here-and-now into full consciousness by means of interpretation.

Interpretation and Its Components

Interpretation is the fundamental technical tool of expressive psychotherapy with borderline patients. Interpretation connects conscious manifestations with unconscious determinants, present behaviors in the sessions with behavior in the patient's external reality and with past causality, and transference with the recalled reality of childhood. Interpretations are verbal formulations of hypotheses regarding the assumed links between conscious and preconscious behaviors and their unconscious determinants. These hypotheses are to be confirmed or disconfirmed by the material communicated by the patient in response to the formulated interpretation. Interpretations and their component features are characterized by interactive processes rather than by isolated events.

Interpretations are most effective when they are presented to an emotionally prepared patient. The sequential use of clarification and confrontation paves the way for an interpretation per se. Clarification, confrontation, and interpretation—techniques that may be utilized in the same session or throughout several sessions—represent the three sequential components of a complete interpretation.

CLARIFICATION

Clarification is the first cognitive step in the interpretive process. Although Edward Bibring (1954) uses the term *clarification* to refer to the therapist's explanations *to* the patient, we use the term rather to refer to the therapist's invitation to and request *of* the patient to explore any data that are vague, puzzling, or contradictory. Clarification has the twin functions of elucidating the specific data and discovering the extent to which the patient understands the material. Work in this area is on the conscious and preconscious level; along with confrontation, clarification is a precursor for interpretation.

Specifically, the therapist will select one aspect of the patient's verbal communication or nonverbal behavior, focus the patient's attention on it, and invite association and further thinking about it. The process helps the patient to bring out new elements of the selected communication, which may throw light on previously obscure or unknown aspects. Clarification may focus on different areas: (a) the transference, (b) external reality, (c) the patient's past, or (d) present defenses. In the following four examples a therapist addresses these areas.

a. I notice that you have been looking at your watch with an anxious expression every time I move my chair. Do you have any thoughts about this?

b. I do not quite understand what made you desist immediately from continuing the sexual play with your boyfriend when he smiled. What do you mean when you say you became inhibited? What did you feel?

c. Am I understanding you correctly that all those terrible fights with your father occurred when you and he were going out alone? Is that a pattern you have noticed?

d. You have been telling me repeatedly that every woman would react like you did, and that you see nothing significant in all those reactions of disgust toward men. What makes you insist on this point?

CONFRONTATION

Confrontation, like clarification, is a precursor to interpretation. Its aim is to make the patient aware of potentially conflictive and incongruous aspects of the material. As the second step in the interpretive process, confrontation brings together conscious and preconscious material that the patient experiences separately. It draws the patient's attention to data that have either been outside awareness or assumed to be perfectly natural but that are discrepant with other ideas, attitudes, or actions of the patient.

In addition to raising questions about the material within the session, the therapist may raise questions about the significance of this material for the patient's functioning outside the therapy. Thus it relates the here-and-now of the therapist–patient interaction to other current interactions. Whereas clarification is purely elucidative, confrontation implies a therapist's decision that certain observed facts are dynamically and therapeutically significant. Like clarification, confrontation can occur in relation to (a) the transference, (b) external reality, (c) the patient's past, or (d) present defenses. The following examples show how the therapist might confront these areas.

a. You have been rejecting immediately—almost without giving yourself time to think—all my observations in this hour, and, at the same time, repeatedly stating that you are not getting anything from me. What do you think about that?

b. I am impressed by your telling me that you shared your new slides with the very person you have been suspecting of plagiarizing other researchers' work.

c. You tell me you felt enraged at your mother precisely at times when she would let you in on family secrets, indicating her preference for you. How do you understand that?

d. The need to search for a new woman seems to emerge in you every time your girlfriend of the moment surprises you with unexpected nice qualities.

INTERPRETATION PER SE

Interpretation integrates and utilizes the information stemming from clarification and confrontation. It links conscious and preconscious material with inferred or hypothesized unconscious functions or motivations. Its aim is to try to resolve the conflictive nature of material by assuming underlying unconscious motives and defenses that, when understood, make previous apparent contradictions logical. The therapist may direct interpretations toward (a) the here-and-now of the transference, (b) external reality, (c) the patient's past, (d) the patient's defenses, or (e) linking the observations of a, b, c, or d with the assumed, unconscious past (genetic reconstruction in the later stages of treatment). These points may be illustrated by the following therapists' statements.

a. I think you have been trying to provoke me into an argument in order to protect yourself against the emergence of sexual fantasies about me. What do you think about this?

b. Your getting tired of your boyfriend, precisely when he seemed so happy with you, reflects a devaluation of him in order to protect yourself from your envy of his capacity to love.

c. Your fear of the noises coming from your parents' bedroom derived from your attributing to their sexual relations the same sadistic qualities that characterize your masturbatory fantasies: you were afraid that your father would damage your mother in sex as you fantasized doing the same in undressing and beating your older sister.

d. Could it be that you are trying to deny the implicit attacks on you in that report because you are afraid of the intensity of your rage against your political rival?

e. Whipping prostitutes and acting tough with me have similar functions: to behave in macho fashion like your father, rather than giving in to your wishes to be taken care of by me and to be sexually penetrated by me. This repeats your childhood wish to replace your mother in your father's life, while submitting to him sexually.

Transference Analysis

TRANSFERENCE

Transference is the experiencing by the patient of affects, perceptions, attitudes, and fantasies in the therapeutic interaction. These do not derive from the therapist but are a repetition of reactions originating in the patient's past and unconsciously displaced onto the therapist. Transferences, in short, are unconscious repetitions (in the here-and-now) of past internalized object relations (in the there-and-then). Transferences are often rationalized by the patient as "realistic" reactions to aspects accurately perceived in the therapist. It is crucial for the therapist to sort out reality from distortion in the patient's observations: transference is the inappropriate or distorted aspect of the patient's reaction to the therapist (Kernberg, 1984, p. 266).*

PRIMITIVE VERSUS ADVANCED TRANSFERENCES

Primitive transferences are rapidly mobilized, highly distorted, fragmented, and ephemeral. They reflect the patient's lack of a stable sense of self or significant others in a variety of situations over time. Any particular primitive transference pattern may shift rapidly into its opposite form or into some totally different form. The therapist may find these transferences confusing, bizarre, often threatening, and difficult to empathize with. Unless the therapist is comfortable with his or her own unconscious processes, there will be a temptation to avoid the experience, either by making premature interpretations (coming to an early forced closure) or by withdrawing.

In contrast, advanced transferences reflect the patient's more integrated, three-dimensional view of self and others. Thus they are more stable, do not manifest the bizarre qualities of the primitive transferences, and can be more easily linked to the patient's past. In all these characteristics they are more consonant with what the therapist can acknowledge within himself or herself; therefore, the therapist's capacity for empathy with the patient's subjective states (the concordant identification in the transference) is greater. Primitive transferences deal with part object relations, and advanced transferences reflect total or global object relations.

*Note that some authorities apply the term *transference* to both realistic and distorted reactions to the therapist.

GENERAL TECHNIQUES OF TRANSFERENCE ANALYSIS

The therapist's long-range strategy for dealing with the transference is to try to diagnose each primitive transference or part object relation, first, in terms of the implied fantasy about the momentary relationship between patient and therapist and, second, in terms of the patient's dominant affect, self representation, and object representation. Often the part self and object representations in a particular dyad are alternately projected onto the therapist, so that for a time the therapist is experienced first as the part object and then as the part self. This alternation makes the interpersonal field of the session confusing to the therapist. But the juxtaposition of split-off representations within the same session sets the stage for more convincing interpretations of the split-off representations: the patient is in a better position to recognize the self and object representations that have been activated. Early in the treatment, weeks or months may pass before the patient is able to fully absorb the interpretation of rapid oscillations in the projected part self and object representations. As the treatment progresses, the cycle length shortens, that is, the patient may understand the nature of the object relationship enacted in the transference more quickly, until the understanding of the entire pattern occurs within a single session. At such times interpretation is particularly effective.

The tactics of transference management in each session are relatively straightforward: both positive and negative transference should be interpreted. Milder forms of positive transference may be left alone, but more primitive, extreme idealizations need to be interpreted because they are the split-off part of negative or persecutory transferences.

Before the therapist interprets the transference, it is important to establish common boundaries of reality with the patient. The therapist should clarify the reality of the situation first and then interpret the unreal aspects of it. The patient's likely distortions of an interpretation have to be included in the interpretation. Acting out, if it does not respond to interpretation, has to be first blocked by structuring (limit setting in the sessions) in order to avoid its secondary gain, and then interpreted.

Secondary gain from transference acting out must be controlled systematically. A patient's relentless attack on the therapist, for example, may gratify sadistic needs to an extent that makes working through the transference impossible: the transference acting out provides more gratification than any understanding or resolution of it might provide.

Given the frequency of condensed aggressive and sexual behavior in the acting out of the transference outside the hours, the patient's sexual life has to be indirectly protected from being overly controlled by aggression. The patient's sexual behavior may appear very aggressive, destructive, and self-destructive, but it is important to keep in mind that sexual experiences also constitute an effort to progress in intimate human relations. Therefore, the therapist must avoid interpreting such behavior as totally pathological. Sexual promiscuity may be an effort to establish relationships as well as being potentially dangerous, and acting out, especially in more advanced treatment stages, may combine defensive and adaptive or growth functions.

Interpretations focus mostly upon the here-and-now as long as transference reactions remain primitive. Premature genetic interpretations may foster intellectualization as a defense and, at times, may increase the confusion between past and present in the patient's mind, leading to transference psychosis (chapter 11).

Primitive defensive operations, as they emerge in the transference, should be interpreted systematically because that strengthens the ego; primitive transferences need to be interpreted first, advanced ones later.

With more integrated patients a systematic analysis of the successive transferences that emerge spontaneously can be carried out, but transference analysis with borderline patients must focus on primitive and chaotic transferences as they threaten the survival of the patient and of the treatment. The primitive transferences are gradually replaced by more advanced transferences, which approach the more realistic experiences of childhood. Then the therapist can shift from the here-and-now to a process of *genetic reconstruction* (tracing the origins of transferences to the patient's past relationships with parental objects).

Countertransference

The term *countertransference* is used in this handbook to refer to all of the therapist's emotional reactions to the patient. Reactions may result from the stimulation of unresolved conflicts within the therapist by aspects of the patient. Reactions of this type are referred to as countertransference in the narrow sense of the term. Countertransference reactions may also arise from the therapist's realistic, conflict-free responses to the patient's feelings and behaviors within and outside the session, as well as to third parties who influence and are influenced by the patient. In addition, countertransference reactions may arise from the therapist's realistic responses to the vicissitudes of his or her own life. But for the most part, countertransference in the expressive therapy of borderline patients arises from the intense, primitive, regressive transferences of these patients and represents the effects of the patient's primitive defenses in the transference.

Although the recognition and management of countertransference are essential to the conduct of any psychotherapy, attention to countertransference takes on paramount importance in work with borderline patients. Because borderline patients use defenses likely to evoke powerful emotional states in the therapist, countertransference reactions often develop rapidly, with great immediacy and intensity. Borderline patients become expert in behaving in ways that elicit unconsciously desired or feared emotional counterattitudes in others. The therapist working with borderline patients must become skilled at identifying and managing his or her countertransference reactions and must learn to rely on them as crucial sources of data for understanding the patients.

Maintaining the Treatment Structure and Technical Neutrality

BOUNDARIES OF TIME, SPACE, AND THE NATURE OF THE TASK

The establishment and maintenance of a stable treatment structure is a prerequisite for the protection of the therapist's stable objectivity, the technical neutrality. It also protects both participants from excessive transference and countertransference acting out. It is essential to establish a treatment frame within which the patient and therapist can conduct their work. Creating this frame includes establishing the space and time boundaries for the interaction, as well as limiting and defining the nature of the task. The creation of such boundaries is particularly important in the treatment of borderline patients because their primitive defenses are chaotic and unstable. Thus, it is essential to establish the location, frequency, and length of the sessions, and to make every effort to maintain consistency in this regard. The patient and therapist should arrive at a consensus about what issues in the patient's life are to be explored and modified in the course of treatment. Treatment goals should be realistic, and the means through which they are to be achieved should be explained to the patient. The responsibilities of patient and therapist should be clearly delineated. For the patient this means not only keeping appointments and paying bills but also being responsible for honest and open communication with the therapist; keeping the therapist up to date about life events; and alerting the therapist to areas of conflict and difficulties that may emerge. The therapist's responsibilities include adhering to the schedule, clarifying in the initial phase how treatment will be conducted, and remaining alert not only to the patient's communications but also to his or her own countertransference reactions (see chapter 3).

TECHNICAL NEUTRALITY

Technical neutrality refers to the therapist's position of equidistance from the emotional forces in conflict in the patient—the id, superego, external reality, and acting (in contrast to the observing) part of the patient's ego (A. Freud, 1936). Technical neutrality is crucial because interpretation of the transference is ineffective without it. Only the therapist who is both a participant and yet a neutral observer, aligned with the patient's observing ego, is able to diagnose, clarify, and interpret the principal active transference paradigm. *Neutrality* does not signify indifference; rather it expresses a concerned, objective, even-handed interest in helping the patient develop self-understanding, without a personal investment in any one aspect of the patient's behavior or interactions.

Maintaining technical neutrality is especially vital for interpreting primitive defenses. With borderline patients, however, technical neutrality is limited by the need to ensure the survival of the patients, those around them, and the treatment process. Thus, the therapist is often called upon to introduce parameters of technique, that is, temporary modifications of technique that move the therapist away from the position of technical neutrality and that are eventually resolved by interpretive means (Eissler, 1953). These modifications include limit setting; establishment of particular conditions for continuing the treatment; and advice and prohibitions, geared to protect the patient's life, other people's lives, and the survival of the treatment. Technical neutrality may be at times dramatically lost, but it then needs to be reinstated. Parameters of technique must be resolved eventually by interpretation so that the therapy can proceed without them. The particular problems that borderline patients raise in the maintenance of technical neutrality, and how to deal with them, are discussed in chapter 4.

CHAPTER 3

Establishing the Contract

Preliminary Evaluation

Before beginning expressive psychotherapy, the therapist must make an adequate diagnostic study to establish the nature of the patient's disorder and the indications for treatment. At a minimum this includes a thorough psychiatric history and mental status examination, as well as contact with previous therapists and treatment facilities. Numerous structured and semistructured interview techniques are now available for discriminating DSMIII personality disorders (Gunderson, Kolb, & Austin, 1981; Loranger, 1988; Millon, 1981). An interview designed specifically for elucidating structural diagnoses, including borderline personality organization, has been presented elsewhere (Kernberg, 1981, 1984). Psychological tests are very helpful in making the borderline diagnosis (Singer, 1977; Carr & Goldstein, 1981).

Apart from the formal borderline diagnosis, numerous features may influence the decision whether to undertake this particular form of long-term, intensive therapy. Ideally, the patient should give some indication of wanting not only *change* but *to change,* that is, of dissatisfaction with something that resides within the self (rather than in reality) and that might be amenable to change with this form of therapy. "Life" goals (losing weight, getting married, having children, making money) are not necessarily legitimate "therapy" goals (resolving interpersonal conflicts, overcoming impulsivity, and so on; Ticho,

1972). Intellectual resources should reflect at least an average intelligence quotient (IQ) and a normal capacity to profit from new learning experiences. Important prognostic criteria within the borderline category include the quality of object relations (demonstrated by the depth of the patient's relations with others as manifested by warmth, dedication, and concern—even given that the patient may present chaotic interpersonal relationships) and superego integration (reflected in evidence of a capacity for identification with ethical values and for guilt as a major regulator). Although the presence of antisocial features does not preclude the patient's benefiting from expressive psychotherapy, it worsens the overall outlook, and an antisocial personality per se contraindicates this therapeutic approach.

The establishment of the therapeutic contract with the patient initiates the onset of treatment, which should not be attempted until the patient and therapist have arrived at mutually agreed upon goals that the therapist feels can be reasonably attained through this form of therapy. Therapy should never begin before the therapist knows what it is for or why it is being undertaken. The stage of evaluation is thus clearly differentiated from the beginning of therapy.

General Orientation of Patients to the Treatment

For patients about to begin expressive psychotherapy, it is important to have clarified the psychopathology and the major issues in the patient's life that are to be explored and modified in the course of treatment. The goals of treatment should be realistic, to be achieved by mechanisms that can be explained to and discussed with the patient; the patient should not assume that simply by showing up he or she will be magically cured by the therapist. It is important to stress the patient's responsibility for honest communication with the therapist, for keeping the therapist well informed about life events, and for communicating promptly and fully about conflicts and difficulties. The therapist's instructions also attempt to indicate the extent of the psychological work the patient should carry out between sessions.

The initial instructions to the patient should convey these expectations and invite free and open communication in the hours, including the proviso that, if no pressing problems, new information, or reporting back are on the agenda, the patient should express freely what comes to mind during the hour. The therapist might say:

We are going to have two sessions a week.* What I expect you to do is to talk as freely as you can about the problems and difficulties that are affecting you at the time of our session; or, if there are no particular problems or difficulties affecting you at the time, to talk as freely as you can about everything that is on your mind.† That may include thoughts and memories and perceptions, dreams and feelings, and questions. The more openly and freely you talk about yourself, the more you try to communicate fully what is on your mind to the limits of your own awareness, the better. When one talks freely about what comes to mind, the important issues tend to emerge naturally. Thus, regardless of whether what comes to mind seems important or trivial, it will help in the long run if you go ahead and talk about it.

My task will be to try to help you gain understanding of the unknown in you. I'll be listening to what you are saying. Whenever I feel I have something to contribute, I'll make a comment. The material with which I work is based on your efforts to clarify to me the known about yourself as much as you can. You'll notice that sometimes your thoughts about yourself will come in the form of questions. I may or may not answer these questions according to what I think is most helpful, so you will notice differences between an ordinary conversation and what goes on here.

Often there is a need to refer back to these initial instructions several times during the early phase of treatment. For example, with the patient who received the instructions just described, the following interchange occurred after the patient had been silent for some time.

Therapist: There is nothing to discuss under conditions where you keep everything buried under silence.
Patient: What do you suggest I do?

*Two sessions per week are a reasonable minimum for this treatment, but expressive psychotherapy may be carried out up to four or five times a week.
†We use this variation of the fundamental rule of free association to minimize the patient's isolating external reality from the treatment situation.

Therapist: Discuss freely here all the issues that are of concern to you about problems in your life. Talk as freely as you can about them. If none of these issues is of any pressing urgency in this session, talk freely about what comes to your mind. I think you remember me saying this when we were getting started last week.

Returning to the original instructions includes reviewing not only the patient's role and responsibility but also the therapist's. During the session just described, the therapist stated: "Let me remind you that my task is to speak whenever I feel I have something to contribute to your understanding about yourself. And that is what I am doing. If I am silent it is because at that point I don't feel I have anything to contribute. If I feel I have something to contribute, I'll say it, sometimes, as you remember, to your annoyance because you feel I am not letting you talk. So, in this regard, this interchange really *is* different from ordinary social interchange."

As part of the initial contract, patient and therapist agree on the fee, the manner of payment, and charges for missed appointments. The therapist offers to try to make up sessions he or she has to cancel and promises to inform the patient well in advance of any planned interruption in the treatment. The confidentiality of the treatment should be defined, and patient and therapist should agree on how the therapist will deal with third parties.

Structuring the Treatment

Although for a few borderline patients these standard introductory remarks are sufficient for treatment to begin, for most such patients they are inadequate to ensure the continuity of the treatment. These patients make clear—through either their presenting history or their behavior in the diagnostic interviews—that their ability to form a therapeutic alliance is severely restricted and their likelihood to act out is considerable. The usual therapeutic environment is not sufficient to contain their destructiveness. Three issues must always command priority: any danger to the patient's or any other person's life, threats to the continuation of treatment, and dishonesty on the part of the patient.

As part of the initial contract the therapist must evaluate whether any of these issues are present. If they are not, the therapist need not suggest them, for to do so might invite further acting out. If they are, however, preconditions and structures for their management must be established.

Features of the contract may run counter to the patient's experience with other therapists; differences must be addressed openly, with recognition of the difficulties they may portend. The patient must get a clear explanation of why the therapist is setting up whatever parameters are required. Agreement between patient and therapist about these preconditions determines whether treatment can take place at all.

A patient who repeatedly refused to leave his former therapist's office and spent much of each day in her waiting room hoping to talk with her between appointments was told: "You will have to leave my office and waiting room at the end of each session. Do you understand why I am saying this, and is this something you feel you can do?" When the patient voiced his uncertainty, the therapist continued: "If you do not leave, I will call for help in removing you. If I have to do that three times, the treatment will end. I shall inform your parents about this so that they, like you, will know in advance that this treatment could turn out to be brief."

Some borderline patients require greater structure than that offered by the usual outpatient or private practice arrangements. They may require psychiatric hospital treatment or an equivalent, highly structured treatment setting, such as a day hospital or residential school.

Borderline patients often have difficulty managing time, which is part of the syndrome of identity diffusion. Thus in the initial contract firm agreements about meeting times and about the beginning and end of the session are important. The therapist's management of his or her time is part of the initial contract: the therapist promises to inform the patient well in advance of any planned interruption of the treatment and to make arrangements for emergency coverage, if needed, during any prolonged absence.

DIAGNOSING THE NEED FOR ADDITIONAL STRUCTURE

The warning signals that alert the diagnostician to the need for additional structure fall into three categories: self-destruction, destruction of the treatment, and destruction of others. The danger of self-destruction is obvious when the patient reports a history of multiple suicide attempts, overt chronic self-destructive behavior, or chronic threats of self-destruction such as repeated hoarding of medication. The risk of danger is heightened when the patient appears indifferent to the consequences. All other aspects of the initial contract are held in abeyance until agreement is reached that the patient will cooperate with the therapist in staying alive.

Potential destruction of the treatment is suggested when the patient sets up treatment arrangements that are predictably unstable. Examples include depending on parents to pay for the treatment while being overtly abusive to them; relying on payment from work-related insurance while sabotaging the job; having seen several therapists at the same time or seeing past therapists while drugged or intoxicated; coming to the diagnostic interviews intoxicated; slandering previous therapists; or having made multiple abortive attempts at therapy.

If the patient has a history of prior violent behavior, or if during the diagnostic interview the subject is preoccupied with attacking the diagnostician while showing little interest in anything else, there will have to be additional structuring. The therapist may say: "You have been violent toward others. I can't do a good job if I'm scared of you. How shall we handle this?"

A more subtle warning of potential threat to the treatment is provided by the following example.

A patient had an excellent relationship with her former therapist until he went on vacation; at that point she decided to stop treatment.

Therapist: Were you angry at your psychotherapist? Why did you stop?

Patient: No, I had gotten as far as I could.

Therapist: You know, it strikes me that after having had this fine relationship with your therapist for three years, you stop the treatment because he goes on vacation. Maybe what might have happened was that you didn't dare to get angry in order to avoid spoiling the ideal relationship you had with him. When he did something that enraged you, you preferred to stop the treatment and keep everything cool, rather than to continue the treatment. If I am right, we would have to keep in mind that if there is a threat of your getting angry with me, for example, because of an extended vacation, you may be tempted to end the treatment with me.

STRUCTURING TO SAFEGUARD THE TREATMENT

When one of these danger situations presents itself, the therapist should proceed in the following sequence:

1. Point out how the treatment situation is threatened by the patient's pathology, specifying the nature of the threat. "You tell me that the only way you can get to my office is if your mother drives you. Yet from what you've said today it's clear that you consistently make your mother angry with you and she responds by threatening not to drive you here. This means that your ability to come to treatment would depend on your no longer making your mother angry, and it is difficult to imagine that's going to happen overnight."

2. Indicate the realistic limitations in the situation, thus eliciting whatever interest and support the patient has in collaborating with the therapist to make treatment possible. In the example just presented, the therapist might say, "What alternative plans can you make to be able to come to my office so as to ensure the continuity of our visits?"

3. Before introducing a structure, clarify what the patient is saying or doing that is causing the therapist to introduce the particular parameter. This sets the stage for the later analysis of the parameter introduced. For example: "By telling me that if you don't return to school you will alienate your family and they will withdraw support for your treatment, you are indirectly insisting that I tell you to go back to school. Why you can't tell that to yourself, but rather insist that I do it for you, is unclear at this moment. It's something we will have to understand. But for now it's clear you have to return to school if you are to be in treatment." Note that in this phase of treatment the

therapist specifically avoids interpreting the patient's behavior. Interpretations are made once the contract has been established.

4. Present an initial treatment contract that protects the stability of the treatment. Ideally, the plan should have the minimum structure necessary to protect the frame and firm guidelines so as to avoid debate with the patient over exactly what constitutes a threat to treatment. For example, if there is a repeated history of anorexia, then the initial contract must include the establishment of a nonnegotiable baseline weight that the patient must maintain in order for the treatment to continue, as well as the procedures for management should she fall below that weight: "Your internist, Dr. Smith, has decided that to protect your health, your weight must stay above 105 pounds. Should you fall below that weight, you will be hospitalized under Dr. Smith's care. I will continue to see you in the hospital" (or "You will be followed by the hospital staff until your discharge").

A patient with known difficulty in paying bills might be told: "It will complicate our work if you go into debt to me as you have with previous therapists. To avoid this, I recommend that you pay your monthly treatment fee in advance."

Whenever possible, the therapist should delegate the limit-setting function to someone else, as this reduces the number of structures that the therapist establishes and therefore needs to resolve later. In the example just given, the anorectic patient's medical management was handled by a medical consultant who bore sole responsibility for determining the acceptable weight level, frequency of measurement, and so on.

Violations of the Contract

When confrontation or interpretation does not eliminate the violation of the treatment contract, the therapist should exercise the least restrictive measure possible—for instance, suspending a particular session, or enlisting the aid of others.

Whenever limits to acting out are set, the patient will be tempted to test them. The therapist therefore should be prepared with a range of responses to intervene with various levels of control. When the situation is not life threatening, the therapist should begin at the lowest level of restriction and then move to higher levels of restriction as necessary. The therapist must be comfortable with the planned limits, for the patient will surely sense any ambivalence. Advance planning to respond to contract violation also protects the therapist from counter-transference acting out. The therapist should also be consistent in setting similar limits with all patients. The therapist who makes an exception to gratify a borderline patient's transference demands may temporarily reduce the patient's demands but risk developing severe countertransference problems. A typical situation is that of the forbear-ing, even "saintly" therapist, who one day suddenly loses patience and abruptly ends a treatment.

The following case examples illustrate increasing levels of restriction. Note that, in each instance, the therapist makes reference to the prior contract-setting session as part of the intervention.

1. The patient, a chronic alcoholic, twice had his previous thera-pies discontinued because he arrived drunk to the sessions. During the establishment of the contract, the new therapist explained that he would not conduct a session with the patient if he came drunk. The following represents a low-level intervention made by the thera-pist during the first psychotherapy session in which the patient appeared drunk.

"As we discussed before we agreed to work together, we cannot have a session when you are drunk. While it is very important for us to understand why you would choose today to destroy our time together, we cannot discuss this while your are intoxicated. I will see you at our next meeting, at which point we can discuss this and any other matters that are troubling you."

2. The therapist of an anorectic patient had in the evaluation period discussed the danger posed by her weight problem. She had presented as a condition for the treatment that the patient contact an internist who would define a weight level below which the patient could not safely drop. The following remark represents a midlevel intervention the therapist made when informed that the patient's weight has dropped below the predetermined level:

"As we discussed before we agreed to begin the treatment, if your weight dropped below 100 pounds, you would need to go into the hospital until your weight returned to a normal level. It is not clear to me why you have chosen at this time to disrupt our treatment. These are important issues that we can return to only after Dr. Jones informs me that your weight has stabilized."

3. The patient had a history of having hoarded pills while in therapy, and on several occasions he had used them in nearly fatal suicide attempts. The initial contract required that the patient bring in all pills he had currently hoarded and turn them over to the physician before any further discussion could go on. Here is a description of a midlevel intervention in a session in which the therapist was informed by the patient that he was again accumulating pills:

"I want to remind you that you are describing a pattern that you followed with your previous two doctors and are now beginning with me. We agreed as a condition of the treatment that the therapy could not go on until you turned over all the pills that you had secreted. I want you to do that now. When you return with these medications, it will be very important for us to look at why you are acting this way at this particular time."

Assuming that the patient refused to turn over the medication, the most restrictive intervention would be appropriate: "As we discussed in our initial meetings, it is impossible for our work to go on if you hoard this medication to use when the spirit moves you. It constitutes so basic a threat to our ongoing work that we cannot continue. Because you refuse to bring in the pills, I can no longer see you. Why you have chosen to destroy your treatment, I cannot say, but that would seem to be an important issue for you to consider. If at some future date you are interested in bringing the pills in to me, then I will be happy to meet with you to review whether we can continue our work."

Behavior that threatens the life of self, the lives of others, or the continuance of treatment constitutes a treatment-threatening situation. Discontinuing of actions that, though destructive, do not pose an immediate threat to the treatment should not be made a condition for starting therapy. For example, it may take many years before a borderline patient with severe obesity can control the obesity effectively; this becomes a matter for exploration within the overall treatment framework. On the other hand, behaviors that traditionally may not be considered destructive qualify as dangerous under our definition. Consider the case of the pathologic gambler. Here the initial evaluation would include an assessment of how much money the patient needs in order to maintain the current life situation, including the psychiatric fees. The contract would stipulate that the gambling could not go to the point of threatening that amount. "Since you tell me that to maintain yourself and your family costs so many dollars a month and your psychiatric fees are additional, you must agree to set aside enough each month for necessities before you can gamble."

Patients' Resistance to the Contract

Borderline patients oscillate between narcissistic expectations—that little will be required of them and much will be given to them—and profound feelings of distrust—with the belief that they will be treated malevolently and must protect themselves from the therapist. In either state patients will feel threatened by the "demands" of the contract and will use primitive defenses to ward off that anxiety. Part of the therapist's task in establishing the initial contract is to confront such defenses.

The patient may challenge the therapist with an accusation: "How can you expect me to change my behavior right away? Isn't this why I'm coming to you in the first place?" (That is, You are being unreasonably demanding of me; it is not I who is asking too much.) The therapist must take up the issue that the patient's belief of being unable to meet the requirements of the contract in no way obviates their necessity. It may simply mean they cannot work together. The therapist might have to say: "While I understand that you tell me you came here because you feel you can't control yourself, if, in fact, you are unable to come to sessions, then I am not able to help you."

Such patients, in insisting that they be taken on their own terms, may be expressing the wish for a magical therapist who can make the impossible possible (perhaps even feeling entitled to such treatment), or may be reflecting the use of projective identification in which their own excessive demands are attributed to the therapist. By making the therapist the harsh, unfair one they defend against their own wishes, now perceived as residing in the therapist.

35

The therapist deals with the patient's objections to the contract by indicating, without reservation or apology, the need for limits and by confronting the patient with how the patient is defending against accepting that reality.

When the therapist attempted to establish the initial contract with an anorectic patient, she complained bitterly that the doctor was making impossible demands. The therapist first stated the reality, namely that in order for therapy to take place the patient needed to have the strength to come to her office. When the patient agreed that she had been so debilitated in her past treatment that she had been physically unable to do this, the therapist went on to confront her with how she had presented the situation: she had accused the therapist of making outrageous demands on her when, in fact, she was demanding that the therapist do the impossible by starting a treatment that was doomed to failure.

At this stage no effort should be made at an in-depth interpretation. The therapist addresses the patient's resistance to the contract by returning to the realistic reasons for the contract, not by interpretation. Interpretive work should be introduced only after the contract has been established. Interpretations presented before the structure of the treatment contract is in place may lead to reactions that cannot be contained. What needs to be said is: "You are expecting me to do the impossible. We eventually will need to understand why it is hard for you to see that there are certain things *you* need to do if we are to be able to work together. Once treatment begins we may also decide to look at what your behavior says about your expectations of me and where this comes from."

Acting Out during the Contract-Setting Process

Resistances to treatment or to the contract-setting process occasionally take the form of acting out during the contract-setting process itself. Such behaviors can range from requests that the therapist intervene in the patient's life before a treatment relationship has been established to behaviors that threaten the patient's life or the potential for treatment. Several brief examples follow.

- A patient telephoned the therapist a few days before their first scheduled meeting, urgently requesting a refill of her medication. She had just run out of her antidepressant and her previous therapist, who had initially prescribed the medication and had renewed it once during the interim, was refusing to renew it again.
- During his first consultation visit, a patient requested that the therapist contact his day hospital because, he explained, the day program would not allow him to register unless they heard from his therapist.
- A chronically suicidal patient gave no indication of acute risk during the initial evaluation interviews. She made an unexpected suicide attempt prior to the very session in which the contract would have been negotiated and reported the attempt at her next session.

Such precontract acting-out behaviors pose special difficulties for the therapist because they take place before the structuring framework has been put in place. The therapist feels powerless, yet responsible. A countertransference impulse to reject the patient can strongly color the process of assessing the patient's suitability for treatment; or the therapist's rescue fantasies may be activated, propelling him or her to enter into a treatment relationship before the contract has been set.

The therapist should deal with precontract acting-out behaviors on a realistic, noninterpretive basis. He or she should act as one concerned person responding to another. The therapist should make clear a willingness to assist the patient in getting the required help, but must remind the patient that they have not yet decided to begin a psychotherapeutic relationship. The therapist should explain that any immediate emergency must be addressed before they can continue to discuss whether psychotherapy would be appropriate.

Acting out that threatens the patient's life or the life of another must be addressed immediately. The therapist should determine whether the patient can control dangerous behaviors during the assessment process. If the patient cannot assure the therapist that control is possible, then the assessment and contract setting should be suspended and the patient referred to a setting where protection is available. In this way, the therapist ensures the safety of the patient but avoids buying into the patient's wish that the therapist be omnipotent. The patient may be told that the interruption does not mean that a decision has been made against psychotherapy, just that the decision-making process must be postponed until the dangerous behaviors can be controlled.

Occasionally a patient will telephone the therapist before a contract has been established to report feelings of wishing to die. The therapist should not attempt to assess the patient's suicidality, because with limited knowledge of the patient such an assessment is difficult over the telephone. Instead, the therapist should help the patient get to an emergency room where such an assessment can be carried out. The therapist may have to call family members, friends, or an ambulance, with the patient's knowledge. In this way the therapist acts as a concerned person who does not yet have a special therapeutic relationship with the patient.

Acting out that may undermine the treatment by forcing the therapist to assume a treatment relationship before the contract is established should also be addressed on a realistic basis. Thus, the patient who requests a prescription renewal could be told that the therapist knows the patient less well than does the therapist who prescribed the medication and that, furthermore, the patient and therapist have not yet even planned to work together. Thus, the patient should ask the previous therapist for enough medication to last until the new treatment has begun.

Throughout, the therapist remains interested in the patient, concerned, and helpful, while maintaining clarity about their current role relationship. In practice, therapists' most frequent error at this point is to make interpretations before a contract has been established, thus sliding into a therapeutic relationship before it has been systematically negotiated. It is crucial to preserve a clear boundary between the precontract consultation phase and the treatment itself. Once a treatment contract has been established and the treatment has begun, the therapist should feel free to refer back to any acting out that occurred during the contract-setting process and to make interpretive efforts to help the patient understand this behavior.

The Goal of the Initial Contract

The major goal of setting up the initial contract is to protect the treatment structure from the patient's destructive actions while permitting a discussion of the patient's controlling and destructive fantasies toward the therapist. Establishing a contract also challenges the patient's distorted expectations of the patient–therapist interaction. If the therapist demonstrates the ability to protect him- or herself and the treatment, it remains clear that the therapist is separate, beyond the patient's omnipotent control, and thus is a potential source of help. Conversely, if the patient is able to control or destroy the therapist (or therapeutic activities), the therapist becomes the pawn of the patient, is perceived as an extension of the patient, and is rendered less effective.

The contract makes clear that the patient bears responsibility for treatment and that therapy is work carried out jointly. The therapist who fails to make clear to the patient that therapy is a collaborative process colludes with the patient's grandiosity ("I can do anything I want to with no bad consequences"), devaluation ("I need do nothing because the treatment is worthless anyway"), or demand for an omnipotent therapist ("All I have to do is show up and you will cure me").

The contract not only challenges the patient's sense of specialness and desire to avoid responsibility but also addresses the health-seeking aspect of the patient, which wishes to join with the therapist. By the same token, the therapist is alloted rights as well as responsibilities. In this way the therapist provides the patient with a figure for identification who, over time, can aid him or her in forming a more realistic sense of entitlement.

Establishing contractual arrangements at the outset allows the therapist to interpret later violations in terms of the transference, thus preempting the discussion of destructive behaviors in nontransferential or extratransferential terms. For example, "Before we agreed to work together we discussed at length your temptation to alienate your parents from you so that they would stop paying your treatment bills. We understood this as a way of destroying your treatment. Therefore, I suspect that your current abuse of your father expresses angry, destructive feelings toward me."

Countertransference as a Complicating Factor

Though countertransference issues abound throughout the entire course of the therapy (chapter 5), they are especially crucial in the contract-setting phase. Management of this first phase can seriously influence the entire course of the treatment; not uncommonly, the therapist's countertransference reactions inhibit his or her ability to establish an appropriate contract. The therapist may be reacting to the patient or to the process of having to set limits. These are intimately connected: the therapist's setting limits can provoke the patient's primitive responses; the therapist's response to the patient's rage, idealization, devaluation, and efforts to control the treatment may influence the ability to set limits.

Borderline patients are extremely vulnerable to dyadic relationships, and can rapidly mobilize primitive transferences that are chaotic, demanding, ambiguous, and oscillating. All these factors contribute to making the initial sessions confusing for both patient and therapist. While the therapist's agenda in the initial sessions is to explore how the two participants might work together, these patients focus on their predetermined ideas about the personality, ambitions, and prejudices of the therapist.

It is no wonder, then, that the therapist quickly develops powerful reactions to the patient. Before the therapist can develop even a rudimentary understanding of who the patient is or what he or she might want, the therapist has been assigned a variety of conflicting, challenging, and changing roles. The therapist may be treated by the patient as the good figure, the bad figure, the one who must make things better, the agent of the patient's downfall, and the last hope. The therapist's subsequent behavior derives not only from what the patient mobilizes but also from the therapist's efforts to bring a premature pseudostabilization to this chaos, at the expense of laying the necessary groundwork for the conduct of the therapy.

The following vignettes illustrate how countertransference reactions interfere with the therapist's ability to use the initial assessment to establish an effective treatment plan.

- In assessing a patient who has a history of multiple suicide attempts and who reports current impulsive suicidal feelings, the therapist does not consider hospitalization as an option, but immediately feels a strong wish to make herself continuously available to the patient to protect him from his impulses. She believes that were he to go into the hospital, the staff would overlook the seriousness of his illness and be less attentive to him than she.

- An abusive and demanding patient refuses to agree to any of the structuring conditions prescribed by the therapist as essential preconditions for treatment. The therapist, though recognizing the need for parameters, is afraid to refuse to treat the patient, imagining that if he did so the patient or the family would sue him for malpractice.

- A well-known rock star with a history of drug dealing, stealing, and lying is referred to the therapist by a well-known colleague. Feeling intrigued by the patient's glamorous lifestyle and honored by the colleague's referral, the therapist agrees to undertake treatment without carefully considering its relative contraindication in view of the patient's severe antisocial behavior.

- A patient reports several abortive experiences with therapists whom he denigrates during the initial evaluation. Without inquiring about the nature of his prior therapy experiences, the backgrounds of his previous therapists, or his understanding of what took place, the interviewer concludes that the patient is not amenable to treatment.

- During the initial interview the patient describes in great detail her promiscuous sexual activity. She is drawn to go alone to bars in dangerous neighborhoods and has been assaulted on more than one occasion during these excursions. The therapist chooses not to confront the patient with the dangerousness of her behavior and does not consider setting limits, but rather spends the remainder of the first evaluation session asking about her sexual experiences.

A therapist who has not resolved his or her own conflicts about omnipotence, sadism, or dependency will have difficulty setting preconditions for treatment as part of the initial contract. Omnipotent countertransference prevents the therapist from recognizing the need for something from the patient. Instead the therapist feels that it is possible—even necessary—to "cure" the patient all alone. Faced with a patient who has a history of being evasive and withholding crucial information in previous treatments, the omnipotent therapist would have difficulty saying, "I insist upon your being open and honest with me if I am to help you."

To the extent that the therapist is entangled in dependency struggles, he or she may be tempted inappropriately to tell the patient, "If you want to kill yourself, don't call me"; in fact, the therapist needs to say, "If you feel the desire to kill yourself, you must take steps to get immediate protection."

The therapist struggling with sadistic impulses may attempt to protect himself or herself by defensively adopting a permissive attitude toward patients. Such a therapist may not be able to distinguish appropriate limit setting from hostility directed toward the patient. He or she will have difficulty saying "If you don't stop getting pills from other doctors, I will have to terminate our work."

Uses of the Initial Contract in the Ongoing Therapy

The therapist may find it necessary to review with the patient the terms of the initial contract at any phase of the treatment, that is, whenever threats to it appear. The therapist should confront the patient with whatever current behavior threatens the ongoing treatment, and he or she must insist that no other issue be discussed until the threat is clarified and contained. After establishing the necessary limits, the therapist should actively explore the meaning of the behavior within the transference. Then the therapist may explore the meaning of the treatment-threatening behavior in the here-and-now of the patient's life. In the advanced phase of treatment the therapist may make further interpretations linking this behavior to its origins in the past.

No therapist can predict from the initial evaluation all the treatment-threatening situations that may arise during the course of treatment. When such an issue arises unexpectedly, the therapist should institute the same procedures that he or she would have undertaken had the information been available at the outset and set about establishing a new contract that will protect the patient and the treatment.

Effective transference interpretations can be made only in the presence of clear and stable treatment boundaries.

Acting out in the course of treatment, as well as requiring the establishment of new parameters and modifications of the initial contract, may also trigger countertransference reactions—especially in the form of tempting the therapist to introduce a parameter without thinking it through. It is wise to avoid sudden decisions, and to plan changes in the contract before, rather than during, a session.

A Sample Case

The following transcript from the first fifteen minutes of the initial treatment session with a borderline patient illustrates many of the principles discussed in this chapter. Though this session focuses on suicide, any threat to the treatment would be handled similarly.

Therapist: Well, so we are starting our psychotherapy today.

Patient: Uh-huh.

Therapist: Is there anything on your mind?

Patient: *(Long delay.)* No.

Therapist: I have been talking by phone with your brother, who called me to tell me that you wouldn't come to the Tuesday session, because you had made a suicide attempt and were in the hospital. He said that he expected you to be here today. Of course, this raises immediately the question about whether you're really being able to go through this. You

Note that the therapist immediately calls attention to the patient's suicide attempt. At this point he is interested only in focusing the discussion on how the patient's behavior impinges on his ability to participate in therapy. The therapist's comment is nonjudgmental in the sense that the issue addressed is only that these actions are incompatible with appearing at sessions. There is no effort at this point to ask about his motivation. In fact, such an effort would undermine the principle being established—that irrespective of *why* he acts didn't call me; you didn't explain anything.

Patient: *(Interrupting)* I did call.

Therapist: You called after your brother talked with me. You told my secretary that you thought that I might be annoyed because you hadn't called. Your brother had told you something like that. So you gave indication that you called after thinking that I might be annoyed. But, um, you didn't call before that.

Patient: I was very out of it *(slight laugh)*.

Therapist: But, but you didn't really take the initiative to start out with, to let me know that you wouldn't show up at your session, at a point when you knew that—

Patient: *(Interrupting)* can I tell you that I didn't even know what day I called. I was very out of it.

Therapist: Well, let me share with you what your brother said. He said that you had been taking some kind of medication or over-the-counter drug, and that's why you conveyed the impression of being out of it. Is that a fair statement?

Patient: No. It was really an overdose.

self-destructively, these action patterns cannot be examined in absentia. Moreover, in pointing out to him that he did not call the therapist, the therapist signals the expectation that the patient has a role in the collaborative effort. Note, too, that the therapist feels free to utilize information from outside sources when there is a threat to the treatment.

Here again the therapist is pointing out his belief that the patient has responsibility.

Therapist: An overdose of what?

Patient: Of Elavil and Valium.

Therapist: Well, that's what I was referring to. So if you were out of it, it was because you had taken all kinds of drugs.

Patient: Right.

Therapist: So I am talking about the decision that you made to take those drugs.

Patient: Hmm.

Therapist: From experience you know that once you take drugs you are out of it and you should have called me saying "I am about to take those drugs and I am not showing up on Tuesday." And you didn't do that.

Patient: It doesn't seem to me to be a normal course of procedure to call someone up and say I'm going to be taking an overdose.

Therapist: Well, then we have to talk about this, because unfortunately that will have to be normal procedure if you want to go through with this treatment. In other words, we have to talk about how we can maintain the regularity of our sessions and, at the same

The therapist here provides the patient with a context within which he can evaluate his treatment-defeating behavior. That is, that he has the capacity to reflect on a body of information known to him, namely his past experience with drug taking, and that he is able to anticipate its effect on him. Moreover, the therapist is stressing the expectation that the patient will use his own reflective capacities.

Again, the therapist's primary focus is on how the patient's behavior threatens his ability to perform the necessary function of coming to session twice a week. The therapist is saying not that the patient has to stop his suicidal behavior, but only that to carry out the

45

time, what our understandings are about your responsibilities regarding your life. For you to undergo this treatment, to come regularly, twice a week, as we are going to structure it, and as we have decided for you to do, it is important that you take responsibility for your daily life. Otherwise you cannot commit yourself to such a treatment. So what I would like to do is to spell out what I see as a minimum requirement for our really carrying out this psychotherapy, and then hear what you have to say about that. OK?

Patient: If you like.

Therapist: OK. We have to assume that you will at some time want to kill yourself. You have acted upon this wish very often in the past. You have been in a coma for days, am I correct?

Patient: Correct.

Therapist: So, these are very serious suicide attempts. They are not just empty gestures, and I think they have to be taken very, very seriously. So what I would expect for you to do is whenever you feel that you are about to make such a gesture, regardless of the reason for it, at that point

therapist's minimum requirement, he must show up at sessions, a fact made improbable if he continues his current course of behavior.

Here the therapist is establishing the fact that there is a shared body of knowledge between the two of them about the danger the patient poses. The therapist makes clear that his concern is not an idiosyncratic reaction, but rather one that the patient could be expected to have as well. This anticipates the patient's narcissistic demand that he be treated in an extraordinary way and saved by the therapist in spite of himself.

you go into a hospital immediately.

Patient: I won't go into a psychiatric hospital.

Therapist: OK, then I won't be able to treat you. *(Pause.)* Then we have reached the end at the beginning.

Patient: And you were the one that said to me that you do not feel that I would benefit from hospitalization.

Therapist: Absolutely sure, but that is not in contradiction to what I said. Not at all. If I thought you needed hospitalization I would suggest that you go into the hospital, but I am not suggesting that. On the contrary, I told you I was proposing outpatient therapy. But what I am saying to you is that there are certain minimal preconditions for carrying that out, and those depend on your willingness to participate, and I appreciate your honesty. It certainly would be much worse if you were not telling me the truth, because that would destroy the cornerstone of the treatment anyhow, while in this way we know where we stand. *(Pause.)* Would you be interested in hearing the rest of it?

Patient: Yes.

Therapist: Um, when you

The therapist is clarifying that he is not omnipotent and that he has limitations.

The therapist describes a range

feel suicidal and feel that you cannot control it, I expect you to get yourself into a psychiatric hospital. Which one, and how, we can talk about. I would expect one of two things, or one of three things. One, if you feel suicidal and you can't control it, you go into the hospital; two, if you already are suicidal and have taken drugs, but are still conscious, you can call the hospital or your family, or a friend, or the police and try to get somebody to get you to the hospital; three, if you decide that you feel suicidal but you can control it, in that case you don't need to do anything. And then we discuss it, and talk about it in your next session.

Patient: OK. What happens if, you take number one, I feel suicidal and I can't control it and yet I do?

Therapist: Yet you do what?

Patient: I do control it.

Therapist: Well, I have no objection to your trying, as long as you are aware of it at the moment when you can't, you have to do something while you are still conscious.

Patient: Fine. What if I . . .

Therapist: have already taken drugs?

of responses, which indicates both his flexibility and his adherence to a definite structure. The therapist is not saying that he expects the patient to be able to control his suicidality, but only that, to the extent that the patient is unable to, he must take certain steps first to ensure the continuity of the treatment.

Patient: Right, what if I already have taken drugs, and that necessitates medical attention as opposed to psychiatric attention?

Therapist: That is a good question. Then you may have to go to an emergency room of a general hospital, where they will first treat you and then transfer you to a psychiatric hospital.

Patient: What happens if I am then stable medically? In any event, must I be transferred to a psychiatric hospital?

Therapist: Certainly. Once you are out of control, somebody has to evaluate whether you need further hospitalization. I am not going to do that.

Patient: You can't do that on an outpatient basis?

Therapist: I will not do that. Once you are in psychotherapy with me my responsibility will be to help you understand what this is all about, and the only way in which I can do that is by staying totally away from all the management and the administrative issues regarding your suicide attempts.

The therapist is doing what he can, within the limits imposed by the establishment of parameters, to retain as great a degree of technical neutrality as possible so that subsequent interpretive work can take place.

CHAPTER 4

Conducting a Session

The initial contract establishes a frame for the work that is to follow. The patient knows what to expect of the therapist, what the therapist in turn expects, and something about the methods to be employed in the treatment. The patient may not fully understand all this, and it may have to be repeated often in the course of treatment; still, the patient begins treatment with at least a cognitive awareness of what it will entail.

Expressive therapy seeks to bring about change by helping the patient to identify distorted and fragmented internal self and object representations and attempts to integrate them into more realistic and stable images. Although examination of current interpersonal relationships is valuable for this purpose, the primary vehicle of the treatment is the analysis of the transference in the here-and-now. The patient's internalized object relations are played out vividly in the transference. As these internalized representations gradually become integrated, the transferences shift from primitive to more advanced forms. When more realistic transferences emerge later in the treatment, the therapist begins to interpret genetic antecedents. Thus over time the focus of treatment shifts, as does the mixture of specific techniques. Yet the approach to any given session remains the same. All sessions are conducted according to a common set of principles which determine how the therapist listens, selects thematic material, and intervenes.

The therapist's basic attitude is alertness to what transpires between him or her and the patient, especially to what is different from normal human interaction. The therapist expects the patient to communicate his or her subjective experience; if the patient does not, the therapist suspects that the patient is troubled by the activation of fantasied, primitive, irrational elements in the interaction. The therapist's attentiveness to such unrealistic aspects is facilitated by the boundaries of the psychotherapeutic situation.

These boundaries include a fixed space, a fixed time, and clear expectations about the tasks and responsibilities of each participant. Protected by the boundaries of the psychotherapy, the therapist will be able to explore personal emotional reactions to distortions induced by the patient; the patient may have gotten the therapist to take on a role that deviates from the usual stance. The therapeutic attitude is always threatened by uncontrollable transference acting out and, at times, by the temptation to countertransference acting out as well. Borderline patients will always attempt to induce in the therapist what they fear and wish to confirm. Paradoxically, the sicker the patient and the more distorted the total interpersonal interaction in the psychotherapeutic relationship, the easier it is to diagnose primitive object relations in the transference.

In general the patient will communicate by both verbal and nonverbal means, as well as by more indirect means through the silent provocation of countertransference reactions. The therapist should try to remain alert to all these channels of communication: content, behavioral manifestations, and countertransference.

In working with borderline patients, even the most experienced therapist will on occasion be in a quandary about what issue requires examination at the moment. The therapist in such situations often feels lost, without a clue as to how to proceed. The therapist should first look to the *content* that the patient is presenting (verbally and nonverbally), asking him or herself whether there is an area of *affective dominance;* if not, the therapist turns next to the *transference* and then to the *countertransference.* If no significant theme has yet emerged, then the therapist should continue to evaluate the ongoing flow of material, waiting until an affectively dominant motif appears. Its absence may indicate that the patient is consciously suppressing important material; if so, the guidelines in chapter 9 are appropriate.

Listening to the Material

In general, the therapist's tasks in any given session are to select the area or areas on which to focus, to explore the chosen topic and, as the treatment progresses into the later phase of integrated transferences and higher level defenses, to expand the stated theme into other areas of the patient's life.

First the therapist must be certain that the patient is communicating openly and honestly. If the patient's communication appears to be false or withholding, *that* becomes the central issue and takes precedence over any other issues except for those that threaten the structure. Therefore, the discussion that follows assumes that communication is honest and open and that there is no acute threat to the treatment.

What to focus on is particularly difficult because the patient usually talks about a number of things. The following guidelines are designed to help identify the dominant subject of the particular session.

LETTING THE PATIENT SPEAK FIRST

The therapist should not speak first and, in particular, should not bring up leftover material from the preceding session unless that material, if unexamined, would threaten the structure of the therapy. For example: "Last time, just as you were leaving, you mentioned that you had lost your job and didn't know how you were going to be able to continue to pay for the treatment. Because that affects whether we can continue to work together, I'd like to hear more about that." Even when the therapist intends to bring up leftover material, the patient should be given the opportunity to begin the session, for the patient may begin spontaneously and may present a more urgent issue.

CHOOSING A FOCUS

The primary sources of data for deciding what to focus on are affect, transference, countertransference, and external reality.

Affect. An issue may be considered dominant if significant affect accompanies the content, or if affect appropriate to the content is lacking due to being suppressed, repressed, displaced, or split off. If the affect is discordant with what the therapist would expect it to be, then the therapist must ask the patient to clarify the apparent incongruity. This can lead to discovering the predominant theme. For example,

"You're talking about whether you should go on living, yet you don't seem to be concerned about what you're saying." When the patient's behavior is incongruent with his or her words and affective dominance is unclear, behavior is probably more important than content and should be explored first.

Transference.   The predominant transference serves as a criterion for identifying the main issue. For example, if in the first ten minutes of the session, the patient discusses how people in authority abuse their power and how the morning newspapers are filled with stories of medical abuse, then the predominant focus would be on how the patient perceives the therapist as a powerful and potentially dangerous person. If affect and transference diverge, that is, if there appears to be a predominant transference paradigm but some other issue is more affectively weighted, then the latter should be chosen as the focus.

Countertransference.   When the therapist is aware of becoming bored, restless, or inattentive, this information is valuable. Assuming, as is usually the case, that the therapist's reaction is not due to the patient's tapping unresolved issues, he or she should ask a question such as, "What does the patient's apparently empty talk (which I have been alerted to by my boredom, restlessness, or inattention) tell me about what is going on?" This question is further subdivided: "Is the patient no longer engaged in open and honest communication?" "Is something that ought to be dominant in the transference being deleted or disguised?" "Is what the patient is telling me not very important or crucial?" The last question can be further expanded by considering these topics: "Is what I am hearing related to the initial complaints or to problems we are now exploring?" "Is it related to our common treatment goals?" "Does it reflect what the patient has done with what we examined in our last session or sessions?" "Does it include new issues important for therapeutic exploration?"

The emphasis on exploring content becomes more important in the second phase of treatment than the first because the predominant communication early on is nonverbal, requiring the therapist to focus on the process of the interaction—"How is the patient relating to me?" On occasion this will be impossible to discern, in which case the relevant information may be, "How am I being made to feel?"

External Reality.   Borderline patients, who have an inordinate tendency to dissociate, often act out important issues in their everyday lives rather than explore them within the therapy. The therapist should be alert to clues to dissociated acting out that may appear in a passing remark by the patient or in information provided by a third party. For example, if the therapist of a borderline inpatient has learned from the social worker that the patient had that morning refused to attend an important consultation, and if the patient does not bring this up, then the therapist should ask after a few minutes why the patient has not been talking about missing the conference. Any issue that emerges in regard to the patient's external reality should alert the therapist to the possibility that it has already or will soon emerge as a transference paradigm. In the example just given, the patient's refusal to go to the conference expressed a fear of being judged; in the transference this emerged through statements indicating that the patient saw the therapist as highly moralistic, arbitrary, and capricious.

The Principle of Priorities

Sessions with borderline patients often appear chaotic; the activation of a number of disparate part self and object representations can lead to the appearance of multiple dominant themes. The appropriate theme for exploration in a given session is selected according to the principle of priorities: behaviors that interfere with an ongoing channel of open verbal communication in the session must be addressed in order of the immediacy of their threat. Thus, behaviors that threaten the survival of the treatment, evidence of dishonest communication, overt breaches of the contract, and enactments that take the place of verbal communication are addressed in that order. Finally, defensive operations within the verbal realm (for example, obfuscation of significant material with reports of trivia, obsessing, and so on) are addressed. Table 4.1 presents thematic priorities. Each theme is addressed with the appropriate technique—clarification, confrontation, interpretation, limit setting, or restoration of technical neutrality. For practical purposes, the sessions should gradually become focused on the exploration of the dominant transference theme. One might consider the thematic hierarchy as the gradual cleaning up of the interactional field in the session, to permit a full exploration of transference developments. In this regard, note that nonaffective themes should be addressed *prior* to transference material because the very nature of the bland and mundane usually serves as a resistance to the disclosure of the transference. Transference themes, however, are not always the highest priority. There are times when intense affect-laden experiences take place outside the direct transferential field (even given the fact that transferential implications are always there); under these circumstances, the therapist should be able and willing to focus on such other affect-laden material, namely, the last item on the list in table 4-1.

Following this principle of priority does not call for the therapist to rigidly ignore secondary themes. In fact, some work with a secondary theme in a session may be helpful in laying the groundwork for addressing the priority theme, as the following example illustrates.

A patient in her first month of treatment appeared after having canceled the two previous sessions. Because missed appointments had undermined a previous treatment, the necessity of attending sessions had been introduced as an element in the initial contract for this patient. Thus, at the beginning of the session, it was clear that a breach of contract was an immediate issue. The patient ignored the matter of her absences but spoke animatedly about how her child made her feel intensely inadequate as a mother. The patient immedi-

TABLE 4.1

Hierarchy of Thematic Priority

1. Suicide or homicide threats
2. Overt threats to treatment continuity (e.g., financial difficulties, plans to leave town, requests to decrease session frequency)
3. Dishonesty or deliberate withholding in sessions (e.g., lying to the therapist, refusing to discuss certain subjects, silences occupying most of the sessions)
4. Contract breaches (e.g., failure to meet with an auxiliary therapist when agreed upon, failure to take prescribed medication)
5. In-session acting out (e.g., abusing office furnishings, refusing to leave at end of session, shouting)
6. Between-session acting out
7. Nonaffective or trivial themes
8. Transference manifestations
   a. Verbal references to therapist
   b. "Acting-in" (e.g., positioning body in overtly seductive manner)
   c. as inferred by therapist (e.g., references to other doctors)
9. Nontransferential affect-laden material

ately shifted to an attack upon the therapist. She said that the treatment was not helping her in any way; the therapist, she asserted, offered no useful advice and provided nothing of any value.

Within the patient, a self representation of an inadequate, empty mother had been activated in relationship to her daughter, who was seen as an ungrateful and insatiable infant. The mother felt depressed and panicky. Early in the session, there was a sudden shift in activated representations. The patient's own self representation was projected onto the therapist, while the patient assumed the role of the insatiable, demanding infant. In the countertransference, the therapist began to question her own ability to carry out the treatment and felt a strong need to confront the patient with her violation of the contract. Such a confrontation, although necessary in this session, could be expected to intensify the patient's feeling of failure and inadequacy.

Several approaches consistent with the guidelines of this handbook were possible at this point. The therapist could directly return to the priority theme of the breach of contract and confront the patient. As the patient reacted to the confrontation with increasing hopelessness and rage, the therapist could examine and interpret the patient's reaction to the initial confrontation. The therapist could hypothesize that the patient was feeling like a failure that day, particularly as a mother, and that she experienced the therapist's confrontation about the treatment contract as yet another demand that she was unable to meet, intensifying her feeling of failure. Thus, the information from the first few minutes of the session could be used to address the patient's reaction to the confrontation of the contract breach.

An alternative approach would be to spend some time clarifying, confronting, and interpreting the projected self representation of the inadequate, empty mother, before returning to the priority issue of the missed sessions. This approach might make the patient more receptive to clarification and confrontation regarding the contract breach. It might also be possible to interpret the patient's absences as follows: she is expressing her contempt for the therapist as an inadequate mother at the same time as she ties the therapist's hands and prevents her from being helpful, thus experiencing the inadequate mother in the therapist rather than in herself.

In the second approach, a secondary theme would be addressed to lay the groundwork for returning to the priority theme in the session. There are always multiple routes to the same end, even as basic operationalized principles are applied.

Thus, the principle of priorities does not dictate the sequence for addressing themes within any given session, but it does emphasize what is most important to be addressed by the time the session ends. In our example, failure to address the contract breach adequately in this session would risk the patient's cancelation of the next session and the possible collapse of the treatment. If secondary themes are addressed initially, the therapist must reserve adequate time during the session to return to the priority theme.

Just as there is a priority for the focus on a theme, so is there a preferred sequence in the use of specific interventions. In general, interpretation is seen as the mutative intervention in expressive therapy. Thus, the techniques of clarification and confrontation are introduced first to prepare for the interpretations that are eventually offered. If acting out may jeopardize the treatment, the therapist should deepen the level of interpretations. If such interventions do not forestall acting out, or if there is no time for such a sequence, the therapist moves to set limits, using the least restrictive intervention sufficient to contain the behavior.

Monitoring the Quality of Communication

As mentioned in chapter 3, the initial instructions to the patient should include the direction to talk about current problems and preoccupations and, if none are pressing, then to say whatever comes to mind.

Once this instruction has been given, the therapist should assess the extent to which the patient is able to carry it out. Patients will follow the instruction to varying degrees; their failure to comply will have a variety of meanings. In studying the nature of the lapse or failure of honest and full communication, the therapist may distinguish several forms of distortion.

1. *Occasional suppression* is the conscious withholding of information with respect to a circumscribed area. In general the patient will be tempted to suppress what is most conflictive, but the positive motivation of the patient will overcome this temptation.

2. *Ongoing suppression* is the patient's systematic, conscious withholding of material over extended periods of time, or the prolonged refusal to speak during most of the session over one or a number of sessions. Ongoing suppression may reflect efforts to control the treatment (or therapist); active competitiveness with the therapist; severe distortions in the patient's ego or superego structure; or other specific transference paradigms, such as severe acute paranoid fears (particularly, psychopathic or paranoid transferences of a pervasive kind, linked to corresponding character pathology; see also chapter 11), or guilt over certain behaviors.

3. *Lying* is an intentional, conscious distortion of reality to mislead the therapist, or suppression of the fact that material is being suppressed. Lying to the therapist suggests substantial superego pathology and should alert the therapist to possible antisocial features. Because interference with open and honest communication undermines the treatment process, any indication of suppression or lying should be addressed promptly and vigorously unless issues directly threatening the survival of the patient, others, or the treatment are present, in which case they take priority.

When the patient acknowledges that there is something difficult to talk about, the therapist should seek clarification at once. The therapist should explore the nature of the patient's assumptions about the consequence of revealing the secrets before dealing with the specific content being withheld. Exploration of the patient's fantasies should be accompanied by confrontation regarding the destructive aspects to the treatment of lying. "Though you are frightened of what I will do with the information, you're also able to discard the rules we agreed on." The therapist should seek to understand the meaning of the behavior in the transference and interpret this whenever possible. Very often there are paranoid fears behind this avoidance which require a long time to work through.

Upon suspicion of suppression or lying, the therapist should not hesitate to present the evidence. The area is then clarified, confronted, and interpreted. On occasion, the patient and therapist may not be able to agree on the presence or absence of suppression or lying, or they may merely identify these behaviors without being able to explore them at the time. In these instances the therapist should label the issue as unresolved and remain alert to its reemergence as the treatment continues.

Suppression often leads to a self-reinforcing cycle in which the initial suppression (or lying) leads the patient to anticipate retaliation by the therapist; this heightened fear of the therapist fuels an increased need to suppress. Chronic intractable dishonesty with respect to central aspects of the treatment which lasts for more than six months may render the treatment impossible.

General Principles of Interpretation*

WHAT TO INTERPRET, AND HOW

The most general principle regarding what to interpret is that what is *dominant* in the material of any session should be interpreted first. This principle corresponds to the "economic" aspects of interpretation.

Interpreting the Dominant Material. The therapist makes a hypothesis about unconscious or dissociated intrapsychic conflicts that may explain the observation. The therapist should not make an interpretation until it is clear that the patient cannot do it unaided. The patient should be first asked how the information presented might be put together. "Can you make anything out of the fact that you came late today, while telling me that you thought about how you wanted people to be angry with you?" Interpretations should stimulate the patient to integrate a step beyond current awareness.

Working from Surface to Depth. Approach the material to be interpreted from the surface downward. The material closer to consciousness should be interpreted first, the less conscious material later (with exceptions to be discussed later in this chapter). In attempting to interpret defensive aspects before content (surface before depth), the therapist working with borderline patients faces the problem of accurately differentiating what is on the surface from what lies below; the

*These rest heavily on the contributions of Otto Fenichel (1941) and Wilhelm Reich (1945).

borderline patient's predominant use of splitting results in alternating defense and content—"surface" and "depth" are interchangeable!

Interpreting Lack of Awareness. Interpretations beyond the patient's awareness should include the reason for unawareness. The rationale for this will be described in a later section, but an example may be useful at this point.

> The patient has been saying that he can't understand why the therapist seems pessimistic about his participation in treatment while he feels so "optimistic." The therapist replies: "One could raise the question whether all along you haven't felt that your life and your treatment were doomed, and whether perhaps you were trying to hide from yourself that concern. What you call an 'optimistic outlook' may be part of an effort on your part to hide the fact that periodically you engage in serious suicide attempts that could have ended already with your death."

Whenever the deeper aspect is interpreted, the patient's motivation for his or her defensive position must be included in the interpretive statement. By providing the patient with an explanation about why it might be necessary to hold such a position, the therapist increases the probability that the patient can listen to the statement and consider it. The interpretation therefore needs to include the recognition that the patient erects defenses *because* of the need to protect against various impulses that seem intolerable, dangerous, or forbidden.

Describing the Conflict. The interpretation should describe the patient as being in conflict. Following the principle that one interprets the surface before the depth, the therapist interprets the defense before interpreting what is being defended against. The surface manifestation is usually more egosyntonic, while what is being defended against is, by definition, less acceptable to the patient and therefore more anxiety arousing.

The last two principles are illustrated by the following vignette. The therapist notes that the patient is silent, and because of the patient's clenched fists and facial expression, believes that her silence is a defense against her rage toward the doctor. The therapist says, "I wonder if you are silent and sitting with clenched fists because you are afraid that if you talk, your anger may emerge and hurt one or both of us?"

First, the therapist is drawing the patient's attention to what she's doing. In this instance he describes her behavior: he notes that she is sitting silently, with clenched fists. Second, the therapist makes a hypothesis about why the patient is not talking—that she fears her own aggression and perhaps the therapist's retaliation.

Note that this process both depends upon and operationalizes the principles of clarification, confrontation, and interpretation.

WHEN TO INTERPRET

The therapist should interpret only when:

1. The therapist feels clear enough to formulate a hypothesis about what the patient is saying.
2. The therapist is reasonably certain that this hypothesis, if shared with the patient, may increase the range of self-knowledge, or, if proven wrong, will contribute to further understanding on the part of the therapist.
3. It is unlikely that the patient would easily arrive at this hypothesis without interpretive help.

Unless these three conditions are met, the therapist should either remain silent or use the techniques of clarification and confrontation. (There is an exception, which will be discussed in the next section.)

Once the first three conditions apply, the interpretation should be made as soon as possible, because in addition to its therapeutic value it offers an opportunity to evaluate the patient's response, which may indicate (1) whether the patient is ready to listen; (2) assuming that the interpretation is heard, whether the patient can do something with it, such as enlarge upon it or make additional associations to it; and (3) how the patient experiences the interpretation—as evidence of the therapist's magical powers, as a narcissistic wound, as a gift, or as worthless.

Faced with a quandary about whether to make a surface or depth interpretation, the therapist should make the interpretation in depth because the patient's reaction will indicate the extent of readiness for this deeper material. If the surface interpretation is made first, the therapist has no way of knowing whether the patient would have been able to work with the deeper level of understanding. An interpretation that is too superficial doesn't lead anywhere; an interpretation that is too deep may at least indicate, by provoking an immediate increase in the patient's resistance, that the therapist is on the right track, and thus may facilitate a modification of the interpretive approach.

Modifying Interpretive Technique for Borderline Patients

ESTABLISHING A COMMON VIEW OF REALITY

There can be no interpretation of unconscious material unless the patient agrees with the therapist on the "reality" of what is being observed. The only distortions of reality that can be interpreted are those that are ego-dystonic.

- A patient has just stated her fear that if she drops out of treatment, her therapist will be profoundly upset and take it as a personal attack on him. If, after persistent exploration of this assumption, she remains absolutely convinced that her leaving will ruin her doctor's life, then it is impossible for him to interpret her unconscious wishes to destroy him. Rather, the task at that point is to work on improving her reality testing so that she can begin to consider the possibility that he might not be destroyed by her leaving. Only then will he be able to explore and interpret why she had concluded otherwise.
- A patient has been describing his ability to take "as many pills as I want without killing myself." The therapist might say, "Are you saying that no matter what you do with the pills you'll be all right?" The patient replies: "No. It's possible that I could misjudge and take too many, though that's unlikely." Having established that the patient does not hold the psychotic view that he is invulnerable to the effects of medication, the therapist can say, "Perhaps you have to convince yourself that you're so much in control of the situation because what you really feel is that you're out of control and won't be able to stop yourself."

Clarification, confrontation, and interpretation are the investigative tools by which the therapist assesses the patient's capacity to test reality. The process may go on in several steps, as the following example illustrates:

The patient expresses the belief that her doctor is interested in having sex with her.

The therapist must first clarify whether the patient is expressing an emotional experience, an intellectual speculation, a fantasy, or a delusional conviction. "Is this an idea that you have about what I might be thinking or do you see me as actively interested in having sex with you now?"

Assuming the patient indicates the latter, then the therapist's next intervention is to clarify the basis for the patient's thinking. "What is there about me, either my words or action, that indicates to you that I want to have sex with you?" The next task is to ask her to reflect on this belief, based on her treatment experience. "Is there anything in our meetings thus far that suggests to you that this might not be the case?"

Then the therapist attempts to assess the degree of conviction with which the patient holds this view. It is important to remember that the amount of credibility a patient assigns to any delusional belief can vary. For example, the therapist might say, "Are you saying there's nothing I can say or do to convince you that I'm not interested in having sex with you?" This could be followed by, "What might it mean that you can think of no way that I could convince you otherwise?"

As a next step the therapist generally will interpret the defensive aspect to see if reality testing will improve. "Could it be that you hold this view of me because it expresses your deeply held belief that men are untrustworthy and interested only in taking advantage of you?" This interpretation is made despite there being no apparent evidence that the patient's view is in any way ego-dystonic; the interpretation constitutes a further effort at clarifying the possibility that, though prior efforts appear to have failed, it is still possible that the patient's perception is ego-dystonic.

If all the above has failed, then the therapist should still pursue efforts to find the point at which the patient's belief is ego-dystonic. To do this, it is important that the therapist keep the inquiry internally consistent with the patient's conviction. The therapist, by becoming even more logical about the patient's belief system than the patient, may force identification of the point at which that belief system is no longer tenable for the patient. Thus, in the example being used, the therapist, staying within the logic of the patient's belief, might say such things as, "Do you believe I would jeopardize my professional reputation in order to have sex with you?" Or, "If you believe this 100 percent, why are you staying here?"

Thus, one proceeds from surface to depth, first testing the limits of the patient's understanding of reality, and then interpreting the inferred defense against perceiving reality accurately. The danger exists that the patient will perceive the therapist's interpretation of defensive denial of reality as a subtle attempt at manipulation. Therefore, the patient's assumption about the therapist's motive for the interpretation has to be interpreted as well. "Could it be that you believe that the real reason for my asking you to consider why you might have trouble acknowledging your positive feelings toward me is that I am trying to get you to like me?"

If, after the therapist has carried out all these steps, it becomes evident that the patient has a delusional conviction (that is, a false conviction that is highly idiosyncratic and motivated, and does not respond to ordinary ways of reasoning), the technique of dealing with psychotic regression in the transference has to be employed (see chapter 11).

MAKING AN EARLY DEEP INTERPRETATION OF THE TRANSFERENCE

Inasmuch as primitive transference dispositions imply a rapid shift to a deep level of experience, the therapist working with borderline patients must be prepared to shift the focus from the realistic here-and-now to the highly unrealistic, fantasied object relation activated in the transference—one that often includes bizarre and primitive characteristics that the therapist has to make explicit as far as his or her understanding permits. Moreover, the therapist should be alert to the danger that the patient may interpret the statement as being derived from a magical understanding rather than from a realistic putting together of what the patient has communicated.

Following the therapist's having made an interpretation that the patient wished to murder her in order to retaliate for severe injustices he had experienced in the past, the patient responded by indicating that he felt as if that meant that the therapist now knew him in a special way that no one before had ever been able to demonstrate. The therapist might say: "I notice that you focus more on your belief that I have special powers, than on any effort at understanding your angry feelings toward me and why they might be present. Furthermore, when I told you about your wish to murder me and why, it was only a speculation based on what you have told me so far. In fact, I can't read your mind; only you can confirm or deny the truth of what I have said."

There are other risks in interpreting beyond the patient's level of emotional understanding: the interpretation may be rejected because it is premature; it may be incorporated in an intellectualized fashion and used as resistance; or it may be used in magical ways. Nonetheless, focusing on the patient's reaction to the interpretation will make it possible to correct such potential misfirings. "Every time I say something to you, you act *as if* I have given you a tremendous gift. At the same time, by your responses I can see that you never pay any attention to what I am saying. All that seems to count is that I give you something, and yet what I give you seems to get lost immediately."

DEVIATING FROM TECHNICAL NEUTRALITY

Being able to diagnose, clarify, and interpret the principal active transference paradigms at each point in the treatment is dependent upon the therapist's position as a neutral observer, aligned with the patient's actual or potential observing ego. This technical neutrality has been described earlier as a stance equidistant from the patient's id, defensive aspects of the ego, superego, and external reality, and close to the patient's observing ego.

Although technical neutrality can be maintained rather consistently in the psychoanalytic treatment of healthier patients, the characteristic tendency for borderline patients to act out in ways that may be dangerous to themselves, others, or the treatment requires that the therapist deviate from neutrality at times. Technical neutrality is, therefore, a theoretical baseline from which deviations occur again and again; it must always be restored by interpretation.

Given the impulsivity, emotional lability, and fragmented sense of self and others that they possess when they enter treatment, borderline patients are at high risk to destroy or severely harm themselves, others, or the treatment. Moreover, the usual supportive aspects of a therapeutic situation (such as the therapist's efforts at understanding the patient, the frequency and regularity of sessions, or warmth and understanding), may not constitute a sufficient holding environment for these patients and, in fact, are likely to be experienced by the borderline patient as intrusive, dangerous, and overwhelming. Therefore, the therapist may be forced to deviate from technical neutrality and introduce structuring parameters to control the acting out. For example: "I think you should go back to school and get your degree. What looks like a surface rebellion is really a self-defeating punishment for such rebellion, and you should not give in to that temptation."

During the time these parameters are in effect, interpretation of the unconscious conflict controlled by the parameters is no longer feasible, but the therapist may go on to interpret the meanings the patient attributes to the therapist's action. This step may initiate the process by which the parameters can gradually be reduced and the interpretation of the original conflict pursued from a new perspective.

Because technical neutrality facilitates the interpretation of transference, it is essential that the therapist, whenever possible, make efforts to reinstate the position of neutrality. In the preceding example, as soon as the patient indicates a willingness to return to school, the therapist needs to acknowledge openly that he took sides in *one* aspect of the conflict and provide the patient with an explanation of why and how this taking sides occurred. In this way, the therapist would move toward a more neutral position.

> "Last month I had to advise you to go back to school and get your degree because at the time it was as if you had deposited in me your own concern for yourself, while at the same time testing me as to whether I would allow you to go down the drain. Now that you're back in school, I think it's important that we discuss *all* your feelings about going back to school, including the negative ones. And I think we should also discuss what it means to you that I should have been put into a position of pushing you into going back to school."

By introducing these parameters of technique, the therapist faces the danger that he or she may appear to the patient as prohibitive and sadistic, thus initiating a vicious cycle of projection and reintrojection of the patient's self and object representations. The therapist can counteract this danger by interpreting the transference, then introducing the structuring parameters as needed, and finally interpreting the transference again, without abandoning the parameters. "I have had to stress the danger to you, in your delicate position in the public eye, of picking up men in your social club. It was necessary for me to warn you about this because at that time you didn't have enough concern for yourself; you needed to test the genuineness of my concern for you and your treatment."

To maintain the optimal degree of inner freedom for exploring his or her own emotional reactions and fantasy formations in connection with the patient's material, the therapist must be particularly careful to intervene—moving away from technical neutrality by establishing parameters of technique—only when the patient's behavior constitutes a threat to the treatment. Otherwise, it is especially important to maintain a consistent attitude of abstinence—in the sense of not giving in to the patient's demands for gratification of primitive dependent, aggressive, and sexual needs within the transference—and to interpret these demands fully and consistently. The therapist's humanity, warmth, and concern will come through naturally in an ongoing attention to and work with the patient's difficulties in the transference and in his or her ability to absorb and yet not react to the demands stemming from the patient's primitive needs.

It is important to avoid allowing the therapeutic relationship, with its gratifying and sheltered nature, to replace ordinary life lest the patient gratify primitive needs by acting out the transference during and outside the sessions. "Though you began the session by mentioning that you lost your job and may have no place to live, you now sit here beaming at me as if all your troubles are over."

The therapist must be alert to this secondary gain of treatment, be willing to interpret it, and, if external limits are required, try to use auxiliary social support systems (a case manager, nurse, counselor, and so on) rather than intervene directly in the patient's outside life and thus lose technical neutrality.

Ending the Session

In general, it is advisable not to bring up new material at the end of the session. Interpretations offered at the end of the session cannot be developed in terms of the patient's subsequent reactions to them or to their accuracy or appropriate level of depth. In addition, the patient needs the time to integrate what has already been presented. Furthermore, the end of the session will often provide important clues about the patient's attitudes toward leaving the therapist and, more broadly, toward handling issues of loss.

The exquisite sensitivity of the borderline patient to loss frequently expresses itself by how the patient handles the end of the session. Whenever possible, the therapist should end the session at the agreed upon time. But the patient often makes efforts to extend the sessions with behavior ranging from bringing up new material to literally refusing to leave; borderline patients may experience great anxiety about the loss of their object or may wish to dominate the object, and thus will create situations that make terminating the session extremely difficult. For example, a patient may wait until the end of the session to announce a particularly potent issue, one that might threaten the continuity of the treatment. The therapist may then feel that there is no choice but to deal with the matter then and there.

> The patient announces at the end of the session that she has decided to take a trip with her boyfriend and that this will result in her missing therapy for the next three weeks. The therapist, feeling that that prolonged absence would be destructive to the treatment at this point, says: "Because you've waited until the end of the session to tell me this, we cannot discuss it during our regular time. Because taking three weeks off at this point, without any prior discussion, threatens our work together, I suggest that we continue this session long enough to discuss why you're doing this at this time. We can discuss later how to handle the arrangements related to the additional time at the end of this session."

CHAPTER 5

Varieties of Countertransference

Countertransference Defined

Countertransference, as used here, includes all emotional reactions the therapist has to the patient. This broad view needs to be differentiated from the narrower concept of countertransference as the therapist's unconscious reaction to the patient. Countertransference reactions may be of several types, which can be classified broadly as "neurotic" or as realistic.

"NEUROTIC" REACTIONS

Attitudes, fantasies, feelings, and behaviors that stem from the therapist's own unresolved conflicts constitute the truly "neurotic" countertransference reactions. These may be further subdivided.

Reactions to the Transference. Countertransference that is counter to the patient's transference. For example: The patient's transference is one of helplessness, viewing the therapist as rescuer. The therapist, because of unresolved conflicts about helplessness, takes over the direction of the patient's life, making decisions for him, or feels angry at the patient.

Reactions to the Patient. Countertransference may have to do with the therapist's transference to the patient as a whole. For example: The therapist treats the patient like a kid brother, putting him down competitively, and so on, and does this *independently* of the patient's transference.

Reactions to the Treatment Process. Countertransference may be not to the patient but to the activity of treating the patient, that is, to the process. This type of countertransference will tend more or less to be manifest in a similar fashion with all patients. For example, a therapist may exploit the treatment process for his or her own masochistic, voyeuristic, or sadistic reasons.

REALISTIC REACTIONS

Responses to the Patient in the Session. Attitudes, fantasies, feelings, and behaviors of the therapist may constitute a realistic response to the patient's expression of attitudes, fantasies, feelings, and behavior; in short, to the intense and regressive aspects of the primitive transference. These aspects of the countertransference are, under ordinary circumstances, by far the dominant cause of the therapist's intense emotional reactions to the borderline patient. They may emerge from any of these sources:

1. In the session (the therapist is annoyed with a patient for continually flicking ashes on the furniture)
2. Outside the session, as a response to a patient behaving in a way that imposes on the therapist's life (the therapist wishes to terminate a patient who repeatedly telephones at home or who manipulates others to intrude on the therapist's life)
3. Outside the session in response to behavior that jeopardizes the treatment contract (the therapist becomes impatient with the patient for his failure to keep a job on which continuance of psychotherapy is dependent)

Responses to Events in the Patient's Life. Realistic reactions to external events in the patient's life (sympathy evoked by the death of the patient's father, for example).

Responses to Events in the Therapist's Life. Realistic reactions to external events in the therapist's own life (the therapist who is about to move to another city may have difficulty listening to the patient talk about separation).

Uses of Countertransference

The rationale for defining countertransference broadly to include all of the therapist's emotional reactions to the patient is that all such reactions constitute important data about the patient's inner experience. Under ordinary circumstances, these various sources of countertransference reactions combine, and the proposed broad concept of countertransference facilitates the analysis of its components. Heinrich Racker's (1968) formulation of two distinct patterns of countertransference—concordant and complementary—is especially useful in explaining how countertransference facilitates the understanding of the patient's experience of self and of significant others. *Concordant responses* are those in which the therapist identifies with the patient's own central subjective feeling state (as when the therapist identifies with the patient's sense of being a victim, so that this feeling of being persecuted may color the therapist's ability to assess the patient's contribution to being victimized). In the case of neurotic patients, the identification is with the patient's dominant psychic structure in the transference: ego with ego, id with id, superego with superego. In the case of borderline patients, the concordant countertransference identification is with their momentarily dominant identification with the self or the corresponding object representation. *Complementary responses* are those in which the therapist identifies with the significant other as experienced yet rejected, dissociated, and projected by the patient. Thus, for example, when the patient is identified with the victim-self, the therapist, in the complementary countertransference, identifies with the object representation, as victimizer. In the case of neurotic patients, complementary responses include the therapist's identifying with the patient's superego while the patient is identified with the id.

Concordant identification allows the therapist to develop an especially fine empathy for the patient, but also runs the risk of overidentification. Through complementary identification, the therapist may gain greater understanding of the significant others, at the risk of becoming less empathic with the patient's present central subjective experience.

The therapist's ability to profit constructively from emotional reactions to the patient depends on learning to inhibit acting on them. A therapist who is secure about not taking action will feel free to use

71

reactions toward the patient as a crucial source of data about otherwise inaccessible aspects of the patient and of the therapist–patient interaction. Utilizing countertransference in this way helps the therapist to avoid repeating with the patient the pathologic interpersonal patterns of the past. By *not* joining in a re-creation of old disturbed patterns, the therapist sets the stage for the analysis of the transference and offers the patient a different object relation.*

The therapist who is unable to accept his or her thoughts or feelings toward the patient runs the risk of denying them or discharging them through acting out. In the service of denial, the therapist may unwittingly discourage any future interactions that threaten to provoke the unacceptable countertransference response, or the therapist may enact the disavowed feelings, rationalizing this behavior in terms of "pathology" in the patient. The patient may respond with triumph or fear to the therapist's efforts to close off an area of investigation, either pursuing the topic with more vigor—thus creating a vicious cycle—or relinquishing any hope of mastery and thus withdrawing.

Whether the therapist acts out countertransference reactions or not, when countertransference is unconscious, the therapist may not be able to distinguish between the patient's reaction to the therapist's reality and a transference reaction. At that point accurate interpretation of the transference becomes impossible. Indirect indications of unconscious countertransference reactions include the loss of ordinary empathy with the patient, overinvolvement with or neglect of the patient, sleepiness, boredom, wishes to get rid of the patient, excessive concern over the patient's instinctual needs, paranoid or guilt reactions, erotization of the relationship, and a sense of paralysis.

Countertransference to Borderline Patients

Several interdependent features of borderline pathology elicit feelings and behavior on the part of the therapist that may make management especially difficult. The borderline patient's intense, usually un-

---

*Analyzing the transference does not necessarily mean making an overt interpretation. It may mean simply that the therapist makes the interpretation silently. Whether or not to interpret the transference aloud at any given moment is a matter of clinical judgment.

modulated and unintegrated, affect states and use of primitive defenses result in the abrupt emergence of chaotic, complex, frequently contradictory transferences, the handling of which is even more problematic because of the generally weak working alliance and the patient's vulnerability to lapses in reality testing. In addition, borderline patients are often expert in behaving in ways that elicit unconsciously desired or feared counterattitudes in others, further adding to the therapist's problems with countertransference.

The patient's intense aggression sometimes causes the therapist to feel as if there is a life-and-death struggle with the patient. Aggression, although it is activated by the transference, is not limited to it, and the therapist often has to deal with aggression expressed both within and outside the treatment hour. Ignoring the patient's aggression may increase guilt feelings and will in turn promote the release of even more intense aggression toward the therapist; or the patient, frightened that the therapist cannot contain the aggression, may flee, withdraw, or become more provocative.

Affect states often appear in unusual combinations. Borderline patients may exhibit intense rage coupled with detachment or glee. The rapid oscillation of affective states combined with the tendency toward impulsivity provoke complex reactions within the therapist.

The use of primitive defenses is another factor contributing to countertransference difficulties. In projective identification, the patient projects unwanted self and object representations in order to eliminate them, and the patient projects valued aspects in order to preserve them. The patient then attempts unconsciously to provoke the therapist to enact the pathologic projections. Because borderline defenses can evoke powerful emotional states in the therapist, it is especially difficult both to receive the patient's projections and to modify them in a therapeutic way.

Consider a patient who projects onto the therapist the role of the abandoning mother: to protect herself from what she believes the therapist has become, the patient withdraws in sessions, speaks little, and rejects what the therapist offers, lest she be "seduced" into the false belief that, because the therapist is momentarily being good to her, she won't leave her. She warily watches for the first sign of abandonment. The therapist, for her part, finds it increasingly difficult to be attentive to this withdrawing, increasingly seclusive, and inaccessible patient. Her mind drifts, she notes that she has trouble understanding the patient's productions, and she is relieved when the patient misses a session. The patient interprets her behavior as a signal of absolute dismissal, feels confirmed in her original judgment, and accuses the therapist of wanting to get rid of her: "When I called to tell you I wasn't able to come on Tuesday, I could hear in your voice how relieved you were. I knew it would come to this." The therapist, feeling guilty because the patient has accused her of something which is to a limited degree correct but of which she has not allowed herself to be aware, readily accepts this global accusation, believing that her own behavior proves that the patient is totally correct. Both fail to recognize that all along it is the patient who has abandoned the therapy and the therapist, refusing to talk meaningfully about anything. Through unrecognized projective identification, both patient and therapist believe that the therapist contains that aspect of the patient that she finds unacceptable in herself.

The other primitive defenses—primitive idealization, devaluation, and omnipotent control—also can induce reactions in the therapist that validate the patient's pathologic view. What makes being devalued by a borderline patient especially difficult is that in the next moment the therapist may be the object of the patient's praise. Compare this to being devalued by a paranoid patient who consistently accuses the therapist of betrayal and whose clear and predictable accusations are less confusing and therefore more easily contained.

Borderline patients often berate their therapist for being insensitive, for not doing enough for them, or for withholding the very thing that will make them better, whether this be medication, additional appointments, physical contact, or other pain-reducing interventions. Their accusations frequently follow the therapist's efforts at confrontation and are couched in terms such as: "How can you make me feel this way? I'm upset enough already!"

Borderline patients may bestow a sense of specialness on the therapist or the relationship, while criticizing previous therapists and conveying that the current therapist is the first one to be genuinely understanding. They may insist on developing a private language, or may express admiration of and encouragement for the therapist's ability to know their thoughts without their having to say much. They may emphasize the union of therapist and patient against a hostile, misunderstanding world. "You are my last hope" is an especially powerful entreaty.

As already mentioned, protestations of appreciation can alternate with expressions of contempt. Borderline patients devalue the therapy through failure to attend sessions, rejection of the therapist's efforts, and statements such as, "Why did I ever think you could help me?" Either therapist or patient may be singled out for devaluation while the other's specialness is retained. For example, the patient who believes the doctor to be extraordinary may wonder, "Why do you, who are so gifted, waste your talents on me?" Meanwhile, the therapist's guilt about his or her emotional reactions is likely to obscure the patient's role in inducing them.

One manifestation of omnipotent control is the borderline patient's attempts to make the therapist an extension of himself or herself. The patient's rage toward the therapist for having a separate life, the confused and confusing identification as both victim and victimizer, the demands to which the therapist has difficulty responding appropriately—all can combine to render the therapist ineffective and make the patient's control complete. At such moments the therapist becomes inept and surrenders his or her therapeutic faculties. Consider the case of the patient who brought little presents to the therapist for his office. The therapist accepted these "gifts" (the earliest signal of countertransference difficulties because it represents a deviation from the frame), telling himself it would make the patient feel more comfortable in his office. After a while the therapist began to feel that the patient had organized the office in such a way that it was more the patient's space than the therapist's.

One way borderline patients manifest their primitive defenses and powerful affects is through self-destructive activity, the most dramatic being suicide (see chapter 9). Uncannily, borderline patients seem to sense the therapist's vulnerability and may choose the exact moment when the therapist wishes the patient dead to announce a suicide plan.

Borderline patients frequently mobilize others to act in ways that cause severe problems for the therapist. Parents, friends, and other therapists may all get caught up in the patient's cause, reinforcing the therapist's self-doubts and adding to the difficulty of clarifying the nature of the problem. The patient may directly invade the therapist's personal life, making public statements about his or her character, criticizing the therapist to colleagues, or threatening the family.

Diagnosing Countertransference

To use countertransference as an effective tool, the therapist must first recognize it and then identify its source.

RECOGNITION

Signals that alert the therapist to countertransference come from actions, fantasies, feelings, and thoughts. Most obvious are deviations from the formal aspects of the contract without prior discussion with the patient. The therapist may suddenly reduce the fee, believing that the patient deserves a reward for working so hard in sessions; or the length of sessions may be altered to fit the patient's immediate emotional state. Or the therapist may be tempted suddenly to abandon interpretation and shift to a nurturing role.

The therapist's attitude, both within and outside the sessions, can reflect countertransference issues. He or she may become inattentive or hyperalert in the session, have trouble recalling previous sessions, or anticipate sessions with excitement. The therapist may violate confidentiality, speaking freely to colleagues and family about the patient, or may become secretive, refusing to write chart notes or to discuss the case at a scheduled conference.

One affective clue may be intense anger that the therapist does not associate with the patient. The therapist may, however, be aware of anger at others, including the referring doctor for "dumping" the case, the family for their lack of support, or the supervisor for failing to provide the correct intervention. Often, this anger at others is coupled with an overly protective stance vis-à-vis the patient.

Conversely, the therapist may express anger by moving away from the patient, rationalizing this as the need to dilute an intense transference. In addition the therapist may withdraw from aspects of his or her own professional expertise (more anger, expressed in this instance through the wish to deprive the patient of the therapist's skill), creating a vicious cycle in which he or she feels depressed, worthless, and incompetent, all of which further contribute to the need to withdraw. The therapist may inhibit interventions out of a vague fear that the basis for the action is suspect. He or she experiences anxiety in the session, in meeting with the family, in presenting the case to supervisors, and in discussions with colleagues. It may not be clear to the therapist whether he or she is protecting self or patient. These anxieties may be called paranoid or persecutory, in contrast to the depressive self-accusations, mentioned before, in which countertransference is colored by introjected blame and irrational guilt.

The therapist may find it impossible to put the patient out of mind, a preoccupation that can be felt as either intrusive or delightful. On the other hand, the therapist may have no thoughts about the patient, whom he or she may confuse with others or think of as a stranger. This may oscillate with the belief that the therapist and patient share a special bond. He or she may anticipate future sessions, looking forward to the opportunity to "get it right" and feeling pressure to make the special interpretation that will dramatically improve the treatment situation. Naturally, such an attitude precludes treating the interpretation as an informed hypothesis requiring confirmation from the patient. Instead, the therapist is likely to insist on the correctness of his or her point of view and to treat the patient's clarifications or amendations as resistances. Frequently, the therapist will think of the patient's behavior as simply willful and ignore its unconscious aspects; or the therapist may focus exclusively on the defensive aspects of the patient's actions, failing to identify strengths or efforts at adaptation. The therapist may come to believe that all the patient's actions derive from the wish to thwart his or her own efforts. These attitudes are especially likely when the therapist closely identifies professional competence with the patient's progress.

The therapist's thoughts can vary from the belief that the work with the patient demonstrates special talents (a variation of the feeling of a special bond) to the more common belief that he or she is incompetent and should change professions. The lack of perspective is extreme when the therapist assumes that this patient provides the *only* accurate reflection of his or her professional capabilities and that work with other patients is not relevant.

Wilfred Bion (1967) has described the therapist's ideal listening attitude as being one without undue memory or desire. To the degree that that position is compromised, the therapist should be alert to the possibility that countertransference issues are impeding his or her functioning. The therapist may come to the session with an a priori judgment about what should take place, allowing no room to learn new information. Whenever the therapist "knows" in advance precisely what has to happen for good therapy to take place, is unable to tolerate surprise, and treats new data with suspicion, it is important to examine these reactions, as well as the patient's role in eliciting them. The therapist may feel cut off from his or her own fantasies and associations, have difficulty listening to the patient, lack interest, and feel bored. He or she may be vaguely aware of efforts to ward off intense affective states and may sense pressure to take action. Any time the therapist is tempted to deviate from the appropriate role, he or she should be alerted to the likelihood that countertransference issues are operating.

IDENTIFYING THE SOURCE

Once the therapist recognizes the existence of countertransference, the next step is to identify its source. The therapist should begin the examination by first considering those situations least likely to be contaminated by countertransference reactions in the narrowest sense. Thus, the therapist should first note whether the patient has invaded his or her life outside the office, as, for example, when the patient is threatening the therapist's family or making demands on the therapist outside the therapy hour. To evaluate whether the reaction is realistic the therapist must also consider whether the objectionable behavior is natural or typical, given the patient's position and life circumstances.

Considering the reaction to the patient's behavior in the session—particularly the reaction to the transference—is a more difficult process. It is incumbent upon the therapist to ask, "What is going on inside me?" During self-scrutiny, the therapist pays particular attention to whether he or she has had a similar response to other patients. If not, or if the reaction to this patient is not easily compared with that to other patients, the therapist is in all likelihood experiencing a problem in countertransference. The therapist may avoid making such a comparison, feeling that the patient is like no other person he or she has ever seen and, therefore, that prior experience must be rejected. Or, though the therapist may want to compare the current reaction with prior treatment experiences, his or her mind may become blank for anything but the immediate experience. The former reaction might represent the therapist's idealization of the patient; the latter, devaluation through withdrawal.

When the therapist is confused about whether the patient is being excessively provocative, a useful question to consider is, "How would a person behave according to normal social conventions?"

Consider the case of a woman who sits staring fixedly at her therapist and states, "There's nothing on my mind." The therapist raises the issue of whether she might be concerned about something that she finds difficult to discuss. The patient becomes irate, shouting, "I already told you there's nothing on my mind!" At this point, the therapist becomes tentative, confused about whether he had the right to ask that question or whether his question indicates that *he* is the one being unduly demanding. Under the conventions of ordinary social interaction, would the therapist's comment have warranted the patient's response? If the therapist judges that his persistence might be deemed inappropriate (that the appropriate range of responses to someone sitting and staring would not include asking her if she was having trouble speaking and, therefore, justifying her outrage), then he should consider the possibility that he is enacting a countertransference theme. If, on the other hand, he cannot see how a conventionally behaving person would react negatively to his intervention, then he can be more confident that countertransference issues do not predominate. However, he would still need to consider what made him doubt his reaction.

The therapist's failure to recognize his response as appropriate may reflect a countertransference problem (in the narrow sense). For example, the therapist who has accepted the patient's idealization may believe that anger is incompatible with perfection and, therefore, deny his rage even when it is perfectly appropriate. The therapist who believes himself to be the cause of the patient's helplessness may be unable to recognize his anger because that would affirm his view of himself as victimizer. At a deeper level, the therapist's own unresolved past conflicts may determine his readiness to respond with unrealistic expectations, temptations, blames, or demands to the corresponding demands made by the patient in the transference.

Leon Grinberg (1979) has differentiated complementary identification in the countertransference from cases in which violent forms of projective identification by the patient bring about complete control of the therapist's emotional reaction. Here the therapist is completely identified with the patient's projected representation, enacting it emotionally without any awareness of it—at least for the time being. Grinberg coined the term *projective counteridentification* for this process.

The Confusion of Self and Object

WHO'S DOING WHAT TO WHOM

The transferences of borderline patients reflect their poorly differentiated sense of self and object (see chapter 6). Especially in the early stages of treatment, the therapist's lack of clarity about the patient's experience of who is doing what to whom accurately reflects the patient's confusion. The therapist's reaction to these confusing, rapidly shifting transferences may include difficulties in complementary or concordant identification.

The therapist who has difficulty with concordant identification intensifies the complementary identifications. For example, the therapist who cannot acknowledge helplessness will have difficulty identifying with the patient's helplessness and is likely to identify with the patient's representation as a controlling object. The therapist who, because of narcissistic temptations, identifies with the idealized object is unable to empathize with a patient's sense of self-devaluation. In both instances the effect is to diminish the therapist's empathic sense of the patient's perception of the self.

Excessive concordant identification produces an imbalance in the opposite direction. The therapist who overidentifies with patients' helplessness cannot help them integrate split-off wishes to dominate others, or help them understand their role in encouraging others to dominate them.

Compounding this already complex picture is the fact that the patient, lacking a stable sense of self or other, continually experiences the self in shifting positions, with potentially sharp discontinuities—as victim or victimizer, as dominant or submissive, and so on. The therapist, in parallel fashion, must struggle to maintain empathy both with the patient's presently dominant state (concordant identification) and with what the patient projects onto him or her (complementary identification); that is, the therapist empathizes with the patient both as all-powerful and as helpless.

BREAKING FREE FROM CONFUSION

To make sense of the confusing self and object world of borderline patients, the therapist must make trial identifications with their entire cast of characters. To accomplish this, the therapist scrutinizes his or her own responses for clues about how the patient experiences the self and significant others. The therapist needs to ask continually such questions as, "Is my feeling anxious now as the patient describes his success at school telling me something about his mother's experience?" "Is my feeling excited about the idea of saying no to the patient helping me understand her pleasure at rejecting others?" Note that the process first involves the therapist's becoming aware of a personal reaction that seems atypical. The reactions are often initially unfocused, and the therapist needs to tolerate the affective uncertainty to remain open to his or her further associations as well as to the patient's ongoing productions. The therapist, as the reaction becomes clearer, attempts to imagine scenarios involving the patient and significant others until one of the players can be understood to fit this reaction. Repetitive efforts of this kind gradually lead to an emerging picture of the patient's internal world of self and object representations in all their contradictory aspects.

At times the therapist may observe that his or her understanding of the self and object representations being enacted in the transference no longer make sense, yet there is no new hypothesis about who is doing what to whom. To resolve this confusion the therapist may find it useful to consider whether the patient is enacting the role of an old object, treating the therapist in the way this object was experienced as treating the patient in the past. For example, the therapist is confused when he hears the patient report victimization at the hands of an "evil" mother, while simultaneously he is experiencing the patient as a persecutor. Who is victimizing whom? By addressing himself to this question, the therapist can become aware that the patient's sense of the mother's behavior is being reenacted in the patient's behavior toward him or her. By developing a greater appreciation of the patient's representation of the mother, the therapist may recognize that he is being put in the position of the patient, who is enacting the role of the mother.

Being in Role

The therapist working with borderline patients must remain open and available both to the patient's transference reactions (which are generally quite primitive) and to countertransference responses while functioning in a consistent, stable, predictable manner according to a definite set of rules. To the extent that the therapist's behavior and attitudes are guided and informed by these rules, the therapist is said to be "in role." Being in role defines his or her functioning for both the therapist and the patient and in this way delineates how his role is separate and distinct from that of the patient. This includes such specific behaviors as specifying the responsibility of each participant regarding fees, appointments, vacations, and maintaining confidentiality, as well as establishing an ongoing self-monitoring system to ensure that the therapist's functioning is consistent with what the patient has been told. In addition, being in role includes adhering to a *therapeutic posture*—a set of attitudes that include maintaining technical neutrality; respecting the patient as the final arbiter of the validity of the therapist's interpretation; listening with an open, inquiring mind; keeping track of his or her own associations and affects; and inhibiting any action that is not in the patient's interests.

In a sense, therapy with a borderline patient can be described as the patient's repeated unconscious efforts to create new roles for the therapist, while the therapist encourages the elaboration of this process in order to be able to examine with the patient the disparity between the role (or roles) assigned and the role the therapist is, in fact, performing. For the therapist to be best able to live with the roles assigned to him or her (and, in this way, come to apprehend the patient's representa-

tional world, both viscerally and cognitively), the therapist must be confident of his or her actual role. Conversely, to the extent the therapist doubts the ability to function in role, the therapist may defend himself or herself against the patient's refusal to acknowledge the transference or disruption of its elaboration, or the therapist may risk being overwhelmed and unable to distinguish transference from reality. In either case, analysis of the transference becomes impossible; in the former because it is denied, in the latter because it cannot be interpreted.

The following example illustrates how being in role safeguards the work:

A severely demanding borderline patient was particularly critical about the therapist's starting the session five minutes late. The therapist noted in herself an immediate wish to explain that her lateness was due to having received an emergency call just as she was about to start the session. The therapist then recognized that her wish to explain was an effort to stop the patient from attacking her and, in the process, from elaborating a central transference paradigm of being unfairly treated. She knew that to act on that wish would be to deviate from role, specifically, to put her needs before the patient's. Instead, she thought about the powerful influence the patient was exerting on her to deviate from role and, in this way, was able to begin to appreciate the patient's wish to protect herself at any cost from what she perceived as the onslaught from her father. That is, the therapist was able to elaborate the effects of the patient's projective identification first (her identifying herself with a guilt-inducing father and projecting her guilty self onto the therapist), and then form a concordant identification with the part of the patient that feared being attacked, and thus to understand the intensity of the patient's need to counterattack.

For the most part, as the therapist's experience increases, being in role becomes almost automatic. At times of stress or confusion, however, the therapist makes conscious use of identification with a set of definite therapeutic principles. The therapist in role maintains ordinary social behavior with the patient but sets strict limits regarding any information about his or her private life or psychological experiences.

In this way the therapist behaves countrary to ordinary social interaction, in which, for example, as a friend he or she might well share private information or fantasies with the other. The therapist's consistent, stable maintenance of these limits to interaction is indicative of being in role. When experiencing the role as a strain, the therapist may function in a severely constricted role, permitting only responses such as, "Why did you say that?" or, "Can you tell me more?" This caricature of therapeutic behavior is a consequence of the therapist's failure to internalize the therapeutic principles. A therapist who behaves so rigidly that he or she appears to be a person without qualities may be unconsciously caricaturing a psychoanalytic stance.

The therapist who becomes aware of blaming the patient can ask, "What is the patient doing that has caused me to abandon inquiry in favor of a censuring attitude?" "What has gotten me out of role?"

The therapist of a Libyan-born borderline patient who had left her homeland at age ten and had spent the next twenty years in Boston threw himself into a study of Libyan culture, looking for clues to understand the patient. He gradually became more and more convinced that he suffered from cultural bias and that the *only* way to understand her was by familiarizing himself with the morés of her country of origin. As he became aware that he was paying less attention in sessions to what the patient was saying and that he was less curious about asking her about her subjective experience (because he already "knew" what she meant through his recently acquired information), he realized that he was no longer in role—that he had ceased to listen with an open, inquiring mind. As he became aware of this, he was then able to understand that he had identified with the patient's view of others as dehumanizing her, of treating her not as unique but as a thing.

Being in role anchors the therapist to the task, offers channels for sublimation, and provides guidelines that monitor wishes to deviate from the role of therapist. This is crucial because the primitive nature of the borderline patients' transference is likely to evoke fantasies in the therapist that can be disturbing, both intrinsically and also because of their capacity to create confusion about how to act. The therapist's awareness of functioning within strictly prescribed boundaries allows

him or her to dare to examine these regressed aspects of himself or herself. It is particularly useful for the therapist to understand that there is no obligation to share his or her fantasies with the patient. Being in role provides a therapeutic context within which the therapist can utilize primitive wishes and fears in the service of understanding the patient.

Countertransference Problems

There will be sessions in which the therapist will be unable to sort out the various countertransference reactions as they occur. Accepting this as normal allows the therapist to take time between sessions to reflect on what has occurred. The therapist who needs to be reassured about his or her sense of understanding may find it difficult to accept the confusion and may feel like a failure for not understanding immediately. The therapist will be unable to use his or her confusion as the starting point of an inquiry for clarifying the nature of the interaction.

Any therapist treating borderline patients must accept that there may be times when he or she will act out the countertransference. When this happens, the therapist should acknowledge to the patient the inappropriateness of his or her behavior as a first step in restoring technical neutrality.

Consider the case of the therapist who, in a session in which the patient has been attacking him constantly, misreads the clock and announces, with ten minutes remaining, that the session is over. The patient accuses the therapist of ending the session prematurely to escape his attacks. The therapist, now aware of what he has done, needs to acknowledge the accuracy of the patient's comment. Only after having done so can he take up the patient's reaction to the premature ending of the session, the patient's role in bringing this about, and his reaction to the therapist's acknowledgment of having acted prematurely. Note that the therapist's acknowledgment of his error is just that. The therapist validates the patient's perceptions so that they can go on with the investigative process. A lengthy explanation by the therapist would constitute an abandonment of his role

as therapist. The therapist would then be acting as a penitent asking forgiveness, making it difficult to pursue what the interaction meant to the patient.

It may well be that, despite all the techniques listed, the therapist is unable to resolve countertransference difficulties. Under conditions of projective counteridentification the therapist may unreasonably feel particularly unfit to treat a patient. At such times, consultations can be especially valuable. The consultant not only provides an overinvolved therapist with an outside perspective but also serves as a transference object for the therapist. The countertransference issues of the treatment are often repeated in the consultation and then can be analyzed. If the therapist finds his or her own resources exhausted and still resists consultation, the therapist may be acting out the patient's demand for a special relationship that cannot be shared with anyone else.

The following vignette illustrates how even a brief consultation can sometimes illuminate the nature of the impasse and permit the work to go forward. It also provides a striking example of the parallel process between therapy and consultation.

The therapist had called for a consultation, stating that she felt she was no longer helpful to the patient. The consultant agreed to a meeting, requesting that the therapist present, without interruption, process notes from a recent session. Following the presentation, they would discuss the impasse as revealed in that session. The consultant stressed the importance of looking as precisely as possible at the clinical material as it unfolded. Within a few minutes of beginning her presentation the therapist reported that the patient had made a reference to "powerful events" from a previous session and had said of those earlier events, "There were two things that stood out for me." The therapist interrupted reading her process notes to say: "Unfortunately, I could only remember one of those things. I didn't know what the other one was and I couldn't bring myself to ask her. I remember feeling somewhat ashamed." Rather than returning to the process material, the therapist went into an extensive discussion of the meaning of her not remembering, insisting that it was proof that she was "screwing up" with her patient.

The consultant reminded the therapist of the structure they had

agreed upon. Rather than addressing the therapist's failure to re-member what the patient had said several sessions before, the consul-tant asked the therapist to examine the meaning of interrupting her reading of the process material and not returning to it. The consul-tant also reminded the therapist that she had originally agreed to present in an uninterrupted fashion. The consultant added that, during the time the therapist had been talking about her failure, the consultant had not been permitted to function as a consultant ac-cording to the established guidelines. He asked the therapist to consider whether she had already diagnosed herself as inept and wanted the consultant to join in the condemnation rather than to assist her in clarifying the nature of the impasse.

The therapist's first response was to feel that the consultant was minimizing her failure to remember in order to save the therapist from facing her incompetence. The consultant pointed out that if what the therapist said was true, the consultant was lying to her and therefore was the one who should feel guilty. The therapist now began to understand the nature of the countertransference. She had stopped reading her notes because she felt guilty about her failure to remember and, wishing the consultant to punish her, had inter-preted the latter's not taking up her memory lapse as evidence of silent condescension. "I thought that when I told you I forgot, you'd criticize me and when you didn't, I thought it was because you felt I was so inept I couldn't do any better anyway, so why bother! Your not picking up on my error meant to me you were indifferent." The consultant, by refusing to play into the therapist's countertransfer-ence, permitted the therapist to recognize what was happening. The consultant had not only refused to criticize the therapist but also had pointed out that if he had been acting as the therapist believed (lying), then it was the consultant who should feel guilty.

As the therapist–consultant interaction began to be clarified, the therapist was able to recall how the patient had repeatedly accused her of indifference. The session in which the therapist was unable to recall the second "powerful event" had convinced her of her indifference and she had felt the need to have the consultant punish her.

The patient's guilt-inducing behavior had inhibited the therapist just as the therapist was attempting to inhibit the consultant. In therapy, the therapist had reacted by feeling guilty—and, in complementary identification with the patient's guilt feelings, had stopped functioning—while the patient was enacting a guilt-inducing authority figure. The therapist now could understood that the basis for her guilt feelings lay in the patient's need to find her unworthy, a charge the therapist had ultimately justified by ceasing to function. This situation illustrates the mechanism of projective counteridentification. The therapist then recalled in the supervision how the patient, while attacking her for being indifferent, had, in fact, been haughty and contemptuous of the treatment for some time, particularly regarding issues relating to the frame. Not surprisingly, the therapist had done the same in her interaction with the consultant, illustrating the parallel process between the dyadic interactions of the supervision and those of the treatment. This allowed the therapist to return to the treatment situation capable of examining with the patient how she attacked her, which led to an exploration of the patient's sense of her own unworthiness.

PART TWO

THE PHASES
OF TREATMENT

CHAPTER 6

The Early Phase: Coalescing Part Self and Part Object Representations

The Task of the Early Phase

Because borderline patients lack an integrated, consistent, and balanced sense of self and of significant others, they misperceive others' intentions and distort ordinary social interactions; their social relationships become exaggerated, unstable, or stereotyped, colored by inappropriate, contradictory, and fluctuating affects. The task of the first phase of therapy is to help these patients to develop images of themselves and others that are multidimensional, cohesive, and integrated. These representations of self and other are formed as the patient gradually relinquishes reliance upon primitive defensive operations and experiences a coalescing of various part self and part object representations. The therapist demonstrates to the patient the part self and object images that are present and the defenses that maintain them as unintegrated fragments of complete self and object representations.

The treatment method employed in this phase derives directly from the object relations–ego psychology perspective discussed in chapter 2. This frame of reference is particularly useful in the early phase of treatment because it provides a clinical structure for organizing the turbulent and fragmented object relations presented to the therapist in the sessions. It is the immediate activation of exaggerated and shifting part self and object relations during the session that contributes to the difficulty in working with borderline patients. An object relations frame of reference facilitates the therapist's work in identifying and interpreting primitive defenses and in assisting the patient in integrating the fragmented representations. In using this approach, the therapist listens to the material with the goal of identifying currently enacted part self and object representations. The next section of this chapter presents one specific method for implementing this object relations approach in the early phase of the treatment.

The internalized object representations of borderline patients are caricatures, that is, fragmentary distortions that exaggerate certain traits and ignore others. The patient's interactions are shaped by fantasized relationships between a caricature of the self (a part self representation) and of the other (a part object representation), under the influence of a particular affect. The therapist's task in the early phase is to identify the predominant part self and object dyads and to help the patient coalesce them into more realistic and balanced internal representations of the self and object.

In order to accomplish this, the therapist first attempts to understand the patient's internal representational world through studying recurring patterns in the patient's interactions with others. Because the part self–part object dyads are mobilized especially strongly in unstructured situations such as the therapeutic hour, the patient's interaction with the therapist provides an excellent opportunity for the identification of the most important primitive object relations.

Within the confusing and turbulent field of the session in the early phase, one after another of the patient's predominant part self–object dyads surfaces. The therapist attempts to identify the part object relations as they arise. To do this the therapist must clarify the patient's attitude toward and expectations of the therapist and of himself or herself from moment to moment. Often several sequences of interaction must be played out before the therapist can recognize the underlying self and object representation dyad.

> Early in her treatment Miss A had great difficulty speaking about sex, feeling that sex was dirty. Clarifications of her perception of the therapist over time gradually revealed that she had come to view the therapist as a strict parent (one part object representation), profoundly disgusted by her body, seeing it as a dirty mess; she, in turn, experienced herself as a filthy, humiliated, depreciated being (one part self representation), who responded with fear and self-loathing to this attitude (the affective link). This view alternated with her view of her therapist as a warm, tolerant, caring person (a different part object representation), while she saw herself as loved and secure in the possibility of freely expressing her wishes to exhibit herself sexually bathing, urinating, and defecating (a different part self representation). In this frame of mind her dominant affective experience was that of being caressed and loved (a different affective link).

The therapist uses his or her understanding to help the patient become aware of the repertoire of caricatures that shape a view of people and that determine a stance in relationships. To accomplish this, the therapist labels the various part self and part object representations that form the basis of the patient's current interpersonal interaction. Corresponding to each interaction in the external world, a particular part self–part object relationship is active in the patient's internal world. This internal configuration may be conceptualized as an unconscious fantasy in which a particular caricature of the self is interacting under the influence of a particular affective state with a particular caricature of the other. Thus, one patient may relate to his therapist in a vivacious manner, talking about material from his childhood that he believes will interest the therapist, and basking in a pleasant feeling during the session. Within this patient's internal world the therapist is the selfish mother who seeks only her own amusement, while the patient is the precocious little boy who has found the secret of amusing her. The affective link is a feeling of security.

It is hypothesized that the internalized representations are maintained in caricature form because recognition of the coexistence of intense and opposing features generates intolerable anxiety. To facilitate the eventual coalescing of opposites, the therapist demonstrates to the patient how the maintenance of the fragmentation protects against this anxiety at the cost of a distorted view of the real social world. This is interpretation of the splitting defense.

As the therapist repetitively works with the part self–object dyads (for example, precocious pleasing little boy ⟷ entitled mother), the patient gradually comes to recognize their influence upon interpersonal behavior. The interpretation of one primitive dyad often leads to the emergence of an opposite (for example, aloof, self-sufficient man of the world ⟷ remote mother). As the treatment progresses, opposing part self and object representations tend to alternate in rapid succession. The therapist demonstrates to the patient that the contradictory images represent distinct aspects of the same object. The optimal moment to interpret the splitting defense is when the opposites actually come to oscillate within the same session.

As will be discussed in more detail, the interpretation of the other major defenses of the early phase—primitive idealization, projective identification, omnipotent control, denial, and devaluation—further facilitates the work. This gradually leads to the coalescing of part self and object representations into more realistic whole self and object images. This work takes place over weeks and months.*

Miss B went to considerable trouble to gain an appointment with a therapist whose reputation she admired. As soon as he agreed to become her therapist, she expressed doubts about whether she wanted to continue in treatment. These doubts focused upon the "little town" where she would have to live during her treatment and where, as she put it, her motivation and interests would be totally destroyed because of its ugliness, provincialism, lack of stimulation, and horrible climate. She described the excitement of life in San Francisco or New York, "the only two livable cities in this country," and raised questions about the professional insecurity of the therapist, reflected, as she saw it, in his remaining in such a small town.

After several weeks, she came to a session elegantly dressed. She told about a former friend, now a prominent lawyer in San Francisco, who had invited her to live with him, an offer she said she was

*The following case was reported by Kernberg (1987).

seriously considering. She went on to describe her current lover as ridiculously inexperienced in bed; she had decided to drop him. She commented that he was a nice but average person, without subtlety or refinement, and poorly dressed. She added that after her first visit to the therapist her mother had raised the question whether she wouldn't benefit more from a therapist who was a younger and more energetic man, and who could be firm with her. The therapist, she said, had impressed her mother as friendly, but plain and insecure.

Asked what her thoughts were about her mother's comments, she said that her mother was a very disturbed person, but at the same time intelligent and perceptive. She then smiled apologetically and said that she did not want to hurt the therapist's feelings, but that he really dressed in a provincial way and lacked the quiet yet firm sense of self-assurance that she liked in men. She thought he was friendly enough but lacked intellectual depth; furthermore, she wondered whether he would be able to tolerate her being open with him. She sounded friendly, and it took the therapist a few minutes to recognize the condescending note infiltrating that friendliness.

The patient then went on to talk about plans for meeting her friend in San Francisco. She considered the possibility that he might fly out to visit her, and she had some ideas about how to make his brief stay in town an attractive experience in "cultural anthropology," namely, the study of a small-town culture.

As the patient continued talking, the therapist experienced a sense of futility and dejection. Thoughts crossed his mind about the many therapists this patient had already had, and how several of these therapists had given a general description of her as incapable of committing herself to a therapeutic relationship. He now thought that she was probably incapable of maintaining a therapeutic relationship with him, and that this was the beginning of the end of her therapy. He felt like giving up, then suddenly had the thought that he was having difficulties in thinking precisely and deeply, exactly as the patient had just said. He also felt physically awkward, and experienced empathy with the man with whom the patient had just had an affair and whom she had dismissed with derisive comments about his sexual performance.

It was only in the final part of this session that he became more fully aware of having become one more devalued man, and that he stood for all the men she had first idealized and then rapidly devalued. He now remembered the patient's expressed anxiety in the past over his not taking her on as his patient, her desperate sense that he was the only therapist who could help her, and the intense suspicion she had expressed in the first few sessions that he was interested in learning all about her difficulties only to dismiss her, as if he were a collector of rare specimens of patients toward whom he had a basically derogatory attitude. He decided that there was an act of revenge in the patient's devaluation, the counterpart of her sense in the past that he would assert his superiority and devalue her. And it then came to mind that he was also feeling much the way she had described herself as feeling when she felt inferior and in despair, when she felt stupid, uneducated, incapable of living up to the expectations of brilliant men with whom she had been involved in the past. He recognized in her behavior toward him the attitude of quiet superiority and subtly disguised devaluation with which the mother, as the patient had described her, made fun of her because of the inappropriate nature of the men she selected for herself.

The session ended before the therapist could sort out all these thoughts. The continuation of the same themes in the next session included plans for meeting the desirable man from San Francisco, the final stages of the dismissal of the current lover, and derogatory comments about the small town. The therapist began to realize that during the last session, this patient had activated in him whatever ambivalence he was experiencing about the town in which he lived. He then became aware that this town also stood for him in the transference, and that the town and himself also represented her own devalued self image projected onto the therapist. Meanwhile, she was identifying with the haughty superiority of her mother. He now thought it likely that she was enacting one aspect of her grandiose self, namely, the identification with her mother, while projecting onto the therapist the devalued aspects of herself and, at a different level, submitting to mother's efforts to destroy her attempt to get involved with a man who might care for her. Now a memory came back to him of her earlier expressed fears that he would try to prevent her from leaving town because of his own needs to keep an interesting patient, and of his earlier interpretation of this fear as representing her perception of him as behaving like her mother, an interpretation she had accepted in the past.

He now said that her image of him as intellectually slow, awkward, and unattractive, stuck in an ugly town, was the image of herself when she felt criticized and attacked by her mother, particularly when mother did not agree with her selection of men, and that her attitude toward the therapist had the quiet superiority, the surface friendliness, and yet subtle devaluation that she experienced so painfully coming from her mother. He said that in activating the relationship with her mother *with an inversion of roles* she might also be very frightened that he would become totally destroyed and that she might have to escape from the town to avoid the painful disappointment and sense of loneliness that would come with this destruction of him as a valued therapist. The patient replied that she could recognize herself as she would feel in other times in what he was describing, and that she had felt dejected after the last session. She said she felt better now, and could he help her to make the visit of the man from San Francisco a success, so that he would not depreciate her because she was in such an unattractive place? She now reverted to a dependent relationship with the therapist, practically without transition, while projecting the haughty, derogatory aspects of herself as identified with mother onto the man from San Francisco.

This case illustrates a typical activation of projective identification, including the projection of an intolerable aspect of the self; the behavioral induction of the corresponding internal attitude in the therapist; the subtle control exerted over him by the patient's derogatory dismissal and self-assertion, which kept him temporarily imprisoned in this projected aspect of herself; and her potential capacity for empathizing with what had been projected onto him because, at other points, it so clearly corresponded to her self representation. This example also shows the oscillation between projection of the grandiose self onto the therapist (when she first began treatment with him), its reintrojection (when she devalued him), and its subsequent reprojection onto the boyfriend following the interpretation. What was projected was a grandiose self representation, although, at a different level, it also corresponded to other objects onto whom such a self representation had been projected in the past.

As long as the part self and object representations are split off and thus unrealistic, primitive, and fragmented, their origins in the patient's past cannot be interpreted. This is in contrast to the ordinary transferences of patients with an integrated identity, for whom genetic interpretations can be made fairly early. The primitive transferences of borderline patients must first be integrated into more cohesive representations of the patient's self and significant others before they can be directly related to their unconscious origins in the past. This integrative process, carried out with respect to the interaction between patient and therapist, results in the transformation of *primitive* or *borderline* transferences into *advanced* or *neurotic* transferences. This is the central task of the early phase. In the advanced phase (chapter 7) conflicts involving the now integrated internalized self and objects are explored and traced to their historical roots.

Miss A, the patient presented earlier, developed a more complex attitude toward herself. She began to see her sexuality and her pleasure in dirtiness as aspects of the same self. Though she came to feel that she could be sexual and yet clean, she retained the idea that she would be hated when dirty. Her more integrated view of herself corresponded with a more realistic view of her father: she now saw him as capable of a wide range of attitudes toward her, depending on circumstances, including realistic and fantasied aspects of his personality such as the sexually seductive father, whose image she had to dissociate from other aspects of him for a long time in the treatment. Here we see the coalescing of the split-off sexual and aggressive aspects of herself and of her father. As the more integrated image of the father becomes consolidated later in the treatment, more classical genetic interpretive work will be possible.

Integrating the Part Self and Object Representations

The part self and object representations are integrated through a process in which underlying representations are identified by the therapist, labeled for the patient, and traced as they contribute to the patient's interpersonal relationships. When the patient has begun to recognize characteristic patterns of relating and contradictory self and object images begin to reemerge predictably, the therapist begins to demonstrate the patient's active effort to keep them separated (that is, splitting as a means to avoid the specific anxiety that would be experienced if these opposing characteristics were perceived simultaneously).

Often the therapist must help the patient to accept representations of self or others that have been disowned. This is done by interpreting the defenses of projection,* projective identification, omnipotent control, denial, and primitive idealization.

For example, a therapist felt paralyzed for weeks with a particular patient who had attacked her for every comment she made and also attacked her for not saying enough. In response the therapist fell into a state of relative passivity. This enraged the patient even more, and he threatened to dismiss the therapist. At this point the therapist recalled the patient's moving descriptions, during the initial interviews, of fear of his own passivity as he entered into depressive states of mind. The therapist pointed out to the patient that he had cornered her into inaction by his repeated attacks whenever she spoke and thus induced in the therapist the very passivity that he hated in himself. Seeing the therapist as passive allowed the patient to disown this quality in himself. This comment, an interpretation of projective identification, led the patient to speak tearfully of his fear of passivity, and completely defused the request for a new therapist. By the same token, the therapist was able to interpret the patient's unconscious identification with her.

The therapeutic method for the early phase may be subdivided into discrete steps, although in actual practice the steps flow one into the other with considerable overlap. In addition, the sequence of steps is not invariable; there may be periods of time during the treatment when the therapist repeatedly loops through a subset of the steps before moving on. Periods of progress in one area may be followed by apparent

---

*Notice that defense interpretations are not restricted to primitive defenses in the early phase; the therapist also interprets the more mature defenses that are operative.

regression, so that the therapist will need to return to step 1 and repeat the sequence.

STEP 1: EXPERIENCING AND TOLERATING THE CONFUSION

As the treatment begins, often as soon as the first session, the therapist working with a borderline patient will become aware of a perplexing, troubling, confusing, and frustrating atmosphere. This experience may be quite distressing, especially because these patients frequently convey a sense of urgency; the confusion exacerbates the therapist's feeling of impotence.

The patient, although apparently intent on seeking professional help, speaks hardly at all, acts as if the therapist has a malignant ulterior motive, berates the therapist, or displays an incomprehensible storm of affect. The patient may make statements that are mutually contradictory or that contradict the current affect or behavior. Such an atmosphere is a hallmark of the early work with borderline patients; *the therapist's first task is to sort out his or her own feeling states.*

Rather than resist or deny the experience of confusion, or attempt to quash it immediately by reaching premature closure, the therapist should experience the confusion freely. In particular, the therapist should pay attention to the specific quality of the feelings being evoked. This may be an important clue to a similar feeling state or complementary state currently active within the patient. For example, the feeling of impotent rage, mobilized in the therapist by the uncooperative yet urgently demanding patient, may in fact represent the patient's own predominant experience of feeling cornered by a dangerously omnipotent therapist. Alternatively, the therapist's feeling of impotent rage may be the complement to the patient's current state of powerful sadistic control.

By not forcing premature closure, the therapist demonstrates the ability to tolerate intense, opposing feeling states. The patient who perceives this quality in the therapist is often reassured, for if the therapist can tolerate the confusion perhaps he or she can tolerate the patient and come to know the patient's internal world.

The following example of the first session of a consultation with Mr. C illustrates the therapist's use of his own experience of a puzzling, paradoxical internal state to help identify an activated primitive self-object dyad.

Arriving for his appointment after having been referred for a consultation by his therapist, Mr. C began by announcing that he really didn't want to be there and didn't think he had anything to say. His attitude was defiant, as though the consultant had just dragged him off the street for a forced consultation. The consultant was puzzled by this defiance: after all, the consultation had been arranged by the patient and they had just met, yet the patient was fighting him off. He was aware also of a strong impulse to force the patient to talk so that he might benefit from the appointment rather than wasting their time. It seemed clear that this would involve a struggle. On the other hand, perhaps he should simply leave; after all, he was now quite clear about not wanting the consultation. As the consultant puzzled over this, he noted that he was experiencing a curiously powerful urge to force the patient to do something to benefit himself.

Deciding to continue the consultation, without acting upon his impulse to tell him that he must talk, the consultant chose to point out that he could not be helpful if he did not know what brought him for the consultation. Mr. C replied that he supposed that on some level he must have wanted the consultation, otherwise he would not have come. The consultant agreed that this seemed reasonable; the patient went on to say that his therapist had insisted upon the consultation because he had become increasingly depressed and had been refusing to do anything that might help him get better. He had been thinking of stopping his treatment. Once, several months ago, he had been depressed and had been given medication that helped him a great deal. He thought that the consultant might recommend medication, especially because it had been so helpful in the past, but he certainly wouldn't take any medication now.

The consultant noted that once again he felt an urge to do something: to instruct the patient to take the medication; after all, it had helped him in the past. He wondered about the source of his urge. Was there a clinical emergency with the patient at the moment? Did he have some need to demonstrate great therapeutic prowess? Could it be that the patient was inducing this urge to take action? As the therapist considered these possibilities, he began to feel that the patient was egging him on to recommend something, only to get into a fight about it. Impressed by the intensity of these uncharacteristic feelings, he recognized that a primitive object relations dyad had been activated. The patient seemed to be provoking the therapist to push help upon him, while he experienced himself as a cornered victim, angrily fending off any help offered by the doctor. At this point the consultant noted a parallel in the patient's report that his therapist was frustrated because the patient was not doing anything to get well.

The consultant responded that something interesting seemed to be going on between them. He felt that the patient had his "dukes" up, ready to fight him off should he try to help. At this point the patient's attitude shifted and he acknowledged that he could see what the consultant meant. He began to talk about himself. Somewhat later in the session, he revealed that he often got into fights with his former wife when he was feeling bad about himself. At those times his wife would try to support him by pointing out his strengths but he would angrily contradict each example she presented. A variant of the same self-object dyad—the angry victim fighting off the helper as though he were an attacker—thus appeared to have been active during the patient's marriage. Moreover, the patient's association to feeling bad about himself suggested the possibility that the activated dyad defended against a self representation in which the patient saw himself as inadequate and perhaps powerless.

STEP 2: IDENTIFYING THE ACTORS

The representations that constitute the patient's internal object world are never directly observable; inferences can be made about the internalized objects by noting recurring patterns in the patient's interactions with others, especially with the therapist.

A useful way of making sense of the overt behaviors is to consider the interchanges as scenes in a melodrama, with different actors playing different roles. The various roles necessary to cast the scene reflect the activated part self and object representations. By imagining the role that the patient is playing at the moment and the role into which the therapist has been cast, the therapist may gain a vivid sense of the patient's representational world. In the earlier example of Miss A, the roles involved were a strict, disgusted parent and a filthy, bad infant; a loving, tolerant parent and a spontaneous, uninhibited child. Further examples of caricature roles are listed in table 6.1.

TABLE 6.1

Illustrative Role Pairs for Patient and Therapist

Destructive, bad infant*	Punitive, sadistic parent†
Controlled, enraged child	Controlling parent†
Unwanted child	Uncaring, self-involved parent†
Defective, worthless child	Contemptuous parent†
Abused victim	Sadistic attacker
Sexually assaulted prey	Rapist
Deprived child	Selfish parent†
Out-of-control, angry child	Impotent parent†
Naughty, sexually excited child	Castrating parent†
Dependent, gratified child	Doting, admiring parent†

*The left column reflects the common self representations, the right column the common object representations; it must be remembered, however, that the role pairs alternate constantly. The therapist and the patient become, in rapid turns, the depositories of part self and object representations.
†Often the parents are not clearly differentiated as a mother and father, but are merged as a single parent fragment.

This list is far from exhaustive; the therapist should formulate a cast of characters for each patient, choosing adjectives to characterize the actors as specifically as possible. In table 6.1, the roles are arranged in likely pairings, but for a particular patient any role could pair with any other.

Given roles are typically played out in alternating ways. Thus, for example, at one point in a session the patient's interaction with the therapist may be understood as the activation of the patient's self representation as defenseless victim being controlled by an omnipotent force, the therapist. Within a few minutes the patient may begin attacking the therapist, berating her, and refusing to permit her to complete a sentence. The therapist now feels controlled by the patient and unfairly victimized. A reversal has occurred. The same self-object dyad is active, but via projective and introjective mechanisms the roles played by patient and therapist have been interchanged. This alternation of roles is often what has occurred when the therapist experiences a sudden sense of having lost the track. When feeling perplexed the therapist should consider the possibility that a reversal of self and object roles has occurred.

To define the cast the patient has chosen for the interpersonal drama, the therapist needs considerable data about the patient's current feeling state, active wishes, and fears, as well as of the patient's expectations and perceptions of the therapist. The therapist gathers these data by encouraging the patient to describe precisely the experience of interacting with the therapist in the here-and-now. This process, *clarification,* involves actively inquiring about the patient's immediate experience and presenting the therapist's view of the interaction for the patient to correct and refine. Thus, the therapist might say to the patient, "Ever since the session began today you have been somewhat secretive and evasive, as though you see me as dangerous. Am I right in this?" The patient's comment might correct the statement and add important refinements: "Why should I talk to you? You never answer my questions but just rephrase what I have already told you." The therapist would then amend the original hypothesis: "So your secretiveness is a reaction to your perception of me as a withholding person. Would that be more correct?" This process continues until the patient and therapist can agree upon the way in which the therapist is currently caricatured, or agree that they cannot agree. The patient's current self-caricature is elicited in a similar manner. Sometimes patient and therapist do not reach agreement. The patient is then presented with the therapist's best description of the relationship with the understanding that, for the present, they see the interaction differently. An effort to understand the sources of their perceptual differences is often quite productive.

Sometimes the patient rejects every suggestion made by the therapist, giving ample evidence in the process that this is done automatically and unreflectively. Such a devaluation of all that comes from the therapist in itself characterizes a primitive object relation activated in the transference. The patient should be confronted with this, and its meaning should be interpreted.

The therapist's internal feeling state is often a clue to the existence of object representations activated within him or her by the patient. The therapist therefore monitors internal states, noticing alien feeling states, urges to deviate from role, intense affects, intrusive fantasies, or wishes to withdraw.

STEP 3: NAMING

Once the therapist has an opinion about the important role of caricatures active at the moment, this is conveyed to the patient. A patient can best hear such communications if they are offered at a moment when the patient displays some spontaneous curiosity about the nature of the interaction with the therapist, and has achieved some distance from its immediacy. (Interpretations are best offered while the patient is emotionally involved in the session, but as the intensity of affect is declining.) The therapist, too, requires some distance from the intensity of the interaction in order to compose a succinct, evocative comment.

The therapist should try to characterize the process as specifically as is possible at the moment, trying to capture nuances that reflect the individuality of the patient. To demonstrate that the process of therapy is not magic, that he or she is not omniscient, and that the patient must provide data, the therapist should show the patient how the characterization was reached. The therapist may say, for example: "You have spoken in an increasingly low tone of voice despite my repeated statements that I can't hear you. That fits my notion that you're angry with me." It is important to include the linking affect as well as the self and object representations involved.

Often a metaphor selected from the patient's own language can serve as a particularly vivid, succinct, and emotionally rich way for patient and therapist to talk about complex self and object images. The following statements illustrate the use of metaphor and simile and the therapist's attempt at specificity in characterizing the active part self and object representations.

- I have noticed that you have been reacting to me as though I am an adversary with total power over you, as if I am your jailer and you are a cowering, defenseless prisoner.
- So I am a stingy, depriving adversary and your only recourse is to act like a word miser.
- Everything would be all right [to you] if I were to obey you. . . . And for this reason I'm like a stubborn child rebelling against a dominant, insistent, rigid mother.
- And you acted as if you had the right to be a child who is not made responsible for her actions . . . where the mother has the responsibility of picking up her child regardless.

The therapist should regard this process of naming roles as the presentation of a hypothesis to be tested and refined on the basis of the patient's response. The therapist will attend carefully to the patient's manifest agreement or disagreement as implied by the subsequent associations. If the therapist recognizes the inference that he or she was incorrect, or even somewhat off the mark, he or she should feel free to acknowledge this and provide a revised impression.

STEP 4: ATTENDING TO THE PATIENT'S REACTION

Having labeled the active part self–part object dyad, the therapist should carefully note the patient's response. Manifest agreement or disagreement is less important than the course of the patient's subsequent associations and any changes that emerge in the nature of the interaction with the therapist.

A correct characterization of the predominant object relationship may lead to several possible developments. First, the self–object interaction just labeled may become more pronounced. Second, there may be a sudden interchange of roles in which the self image just named is projected onto the therapist and the object image is reintrojected into the patient. Thus, the patient who has just been described as a controlling mother treating the therapist as a naughty but defenseless child may feel defenseless and criticized by an all-powerful therapist-mother. The third outcome of a correct characterization would be evidence of insight. The patient might acknowledge with an emotional conviction recognition of what the therapist is describing, and may spontaneously describe other interactions demonstrating a similar pattern. A correct characterization may lead to previously unreported material or to new memories that are linked to the described self-object dyad. A fourth outcome might be the sudden activation of a different object relations dyad. Finally, a correct naming of roles might be met by blanket denial.

Incorrect naming of roles may lead to overt disagreement, blanket denial, or even acknowledged agreement emerging from an effort to please the therapist. The patient may respond with relief if an inexact characterization organizes a previously chaotic experience—even the incorrect formulation may be taken by the patient as a gift from the therapist, as a token of the therapist's belief that understanding is possible; on the other hand, the patient may react with dismay, realizing that the therapist cannot always understand, is not omniscient, and is separate. Thus, one may not immediately be able to assess the correctness of the intervention. In such situations the therapist should continue to entertain the possibility of being incorrect and should listen patiently as additional material emerges to confirm or refute the hypothesis. Sometimes the therapist will need to tolerate such uncertainty for a long time.

As the treatment progresses, correct interventions will more often lead to shifts away from the described dyad and toward activation of an opposite dyad. Opposing self images and opposing object images thus may emerge within the same session. When this occurs, an interpretation of splitting may be most meaningful to the patient.

For example, when the patient has reacted to the therapist as a cold, distant parent at one point in the session and as a warm and loving parent at another point, the therapist may point out how feelings toward the therapist-mother as a hateful, cold witch have been kept separate from feelings of him as a nurturant mother in order to avoid harboring hate for one who is loved—a state that would produce intolerable anxiety. Correct interpretations of the object relationships do not lead to insight the first several times they are offered; repeated interpretations as the same pattern recurs are typically required.

STEP 5: INTERPRETING PRIMITIVE DEFENSES

All defenses are mechanisms for avoiding intolerable intrapsychic conflict. Primitive defenses are mechanisms that attempt such avoidance by sharp, unrealistic separation between loving and hateful aspects of one's self and others, so that even if both of these contradictory affects appear in consciousness, they do so in total separation. Splitting, the central mechanism of the primitive defenses, isolates aspects of the self or object. Omnipotent control, projective identification, primitive idealization, devaluation, and denial make it possible to sustain splitting through the belief that unacceptable aspects of the self are present in others instead, that bad objects are good ones, and that the contradictions are of no emotional consequence.

To bring the part self and object representation to the patient's awareness, the therapist often must retrieve them from their projected locations. This is done by demonstrating the use of such defenses as projective identification, omnipotent control, and projection. Similarly, the use of primitive idealization, devaluation, and denial are interpreted to aid the patient in recognizing the true valence (good, bad, or mixed) of the self and object images.

Once the therapist has demonstrated the repertoire of caricatures that influence the patient's relationships (steps 3 and 4), the next task is to bring together the self and object fragments. This is when the interpretation of primitive defenses is most useful. We will discuss each primitive defense below.

Splitting. The clearest manifestation of splitting is seen in the patient's perception of the therapist or the self as all good or all bad, with the concomitant possibility of a complete, abrupt reversal of all the relevant feelings and conceptualizations. Sudden shifts in the patient's perception of the therapist or self or a complete separation of contradictory reactions to the same transference theme are manifestations of splitting mechanisms.

Therapist: Right now you're telling me I'm benevolent and you are totally relaxed with me.

Patient: What's wrong with that?

Therapist: I find it puzzling that ten minutes ago you said you had to "watch me like a hawk," that I was dangerous.

Patient: That's how you were *then*. You're different now.

Therapist: How can we make sense out of my apparently changing so quickly? It's as if you know what to do with me only when you see me as at one extreme or the other.

Primitive Idealization. Primitive idealization, omnipotence, and devaluation all derive from splitting. Primitive idealization complicates the tendency to see external objects as either totally good or totally bad by artificially and pathologically increasing their quality of goodness or badness.

Primitive idealization creates unrealistic, all good and powerful images, reflected in the patient's treating the therapist as an ideal, omnipotent, or godly figure on whom he or she can depend unquestioningly. The therapist may be seen as a potential ally against equally powerful (and equally unrealistic) all bad objects within the patient.

Omnipotence and Devaluation. Omnipotence and devaluation, like idealization, affect both self and object representations. Typically, borderline patients represent themselves in a highly inflated, grandiose way while treating the therapist in a depreciating, emotionally degrading fashion, although the reverse can also occur. In the early phase frequently there is a shift back and forth from one position to the other.

Projective Identification. As was pointed out in chapter 1, in contrast to higher levels of projection—which are characterized by attributing to another an impulse repressed in oneself—primitive forms of projection, particularly projective identification, are characterized by (1) the tendency to continue to experience the impulse that is simultaneously being projected onto the other person, (2) fear of the other person now seen under the influence of that projected impulse, (3) the need, therefore, to control the other person, and (4) an unconscious tendency to arouse the feared and projected identification in the other person. Projective identification, therefore, implies interactions, and this may be reflected dramatically in the transference.

The patient who is attempting to induce a certain reaction in the therapist may accuse the therapist of having that reaction. For example, the patient accuses the therapist of being sadistic while treating the therapist in a cold, controlling, derogatory way, and at the same time feeling the need to defend against him or her.

Denial. Denial in borderline patients reinforces the splitting process. These patients can remember perceptions, thoughts, and feelings about themselves or other people completely opposite to those experienced at the moment, but this memory has no emotional relevance and cannot influence the way they feel now. Denial may be manifested by lack of appropriate emotional reaction to an immediate, serious, pressing need, conflict, or danger. The patient calmly conveys cognitive awareness of the situation while denying its emotional implications, or shuts out an entire area from awareness, thus "protecting" against a potential area of conflict.

Systematic interpretation of the primitive defenses leads to shifts in the object relations activated in the session. Such shifts are valuable in confirming the accuracy of the therapist's interpretations. The patient gradually becomes aware of contradictory internalized object images. When whole, three-dimensional internalized self and object representations have been formed, the patient has entered the more advanced phase of treatment.

Figure 6.1 presents an overview of the key processes of the early phase.

FIGURE 6.1
The Interpretive Transformation of Primitive Object Relations Expressed in the Transference

Stage 1: The Initial Chaos in the Session

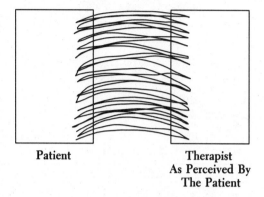

Patient   **Therapist As Perceived By The Patient**

Fragmented part self and object representations are activated in rapid succession, bombarding the therapist with chaotic and contradictory object relations. The central task is to tolerate the confusion, accept the uncertainty, and refrain from overactivity (step 1 of the technique).

Stage 2: Identifying the Dominant Transference Self-Object Dyad

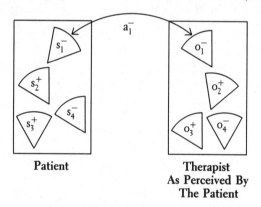

Patient   **Therapist As Perceived By The Patient**

A dominant dyad of the self and of the therapist in interaction becomes apparent. The therapeutic task is first to identify the part self and object representations and their linking affect and then to interpret this. The transference interpretation includes the naming of the active part self and part object representations and their affective link. This is offered to the patient as the therapist's best hypothesis, subject to correction and refinement (steps 2 and 3 of the technique).

Key: ☐ Attributions by patient to self and therapist.
    ▽ Part representation
    s Part self representation (numbered by subscripts)
    o Part object representation (numbered by subscripts)
    a Linking affect (numbered by subscripts)
    + Affectively positive
    − Affectively negative

Stage 3: The Post-interpretation Object Field

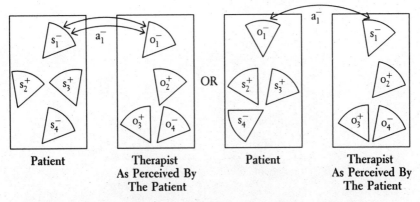

| Patient | Therapist
As Perceived By
The Patient | Patient | Therapist
As Perceived By
The Patient |

Following the interpretations, the therapist observes changes in the self and object representations that are active, or changes in affective intensity. Such shifts are a more reliable indicator of the correctness of the interpretation than is the patient's conscious acceptance or rejection of the interpretive content. Often a correct interpretation of an activated object relation is followed either by an intensification of the same pattern or by an exchange of the projected and introjected components so that the previously activated self image is now projected onto the therapist and the object image is now activated within the self. When an exchange of self and object representations has occurred, interpretation of this process is indicated (step 4 of the technique).

Stage 4: Incorporation of Both Components of the Dyad

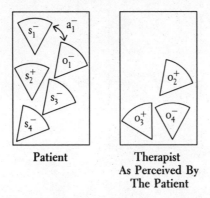

| Patient | Therapist
As Perceived By
The Patient |

With repetitive interpretative work, the patient comes to recognize that both the self and object part representations originate from within. Interpretation of the defense of projective identification facilitates the emergence of this stage. The therapist is perceived as separate, having his or her own qualities, good or bad, but still within a part object relationship.

Stage 5: Integration of Opposites

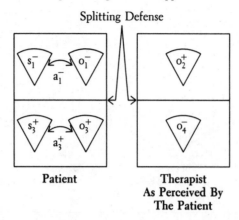

Patient

Therapist
As Perceived By
The Patient

Stages 1 through 4 have been carried out also for part self and part object dyads of the opposite affective valence to those indicated above. Interpretation of the splitting of the good and bad self and object representations allows their coalescing into more complete representations (step 5 of the technique).

Stage 6: Entry into Advanced Phase

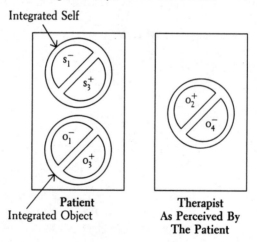

Integrated Object

Patient

Therapist
As Perceived By
The Patient

The patient has begun to integrate the contradictory part self and part object representations and develops a more balanced and three-dimensional view of self and object. The classical tripartite structure now develops.

Interpreting During the Early Phase

In addressing the tasks of the early phase, the therapist makes extensive use of clarification, confrontation, and interpretation. In early-phase work with borderline patients some modifications in emphasis and timing are important. We present these as the following guidelines.

AVOIDING GENETIC INTERPRETATIONS

The lack of integration of the self-concept and the lack of differentiation and individualization of object representations interfere with borderline patients' ability to distinguish present and past object relations. They confuse transference and reality and fail to differentiate the therapist from the transference object. For example, "You react to me this way because you see in me your mother's attitude in your past" may be responded to by the patient as though the therapist had asserted, "It is terrible that, having had such a mother, you now have a therapist exactly like her." In other words, the genetic interpretation is misinterpreted as a confirmation that the therapist is really like mother, that both of them are really dangerous enemies; past and present become confused in the patient's mind. Therefore, full genetic reconstruction must await the next stage of the treatment.

DEALING WITH THE NEGATIVE TRANSFERENCE

Dealing directly with the borderline patient's primitive conflicts about aggression and intolerance of ambivalent feelings is the major vehicle for indirectly strengthening the therapeutic alliance. The analysis of the negative transference allows for the emergence of more positive feelings in the transference and for the development of ambivalence. The negative transference should be interpreted as fully as possible and, as is true of all the material interpreted during this phase, should be systematically elaborated only in the here-and-now.

It is important to be alert to the beginnings of ambivalence in the face of apparently unambivalent hostility. Generally, the more positive aspects are demonstrated in the patient's behavior and, because of the effectiveness of the primitive defenses, do not create any sense of conflict about the seemingly absolute negative position the patient is taking. Pointing to the positive aspects may mitigate the patient's sense of being all bad. If positive aspects are not acknowledged, the necessary emphasis upon the negative transference may perpetuate the patient's perception of the self as totally bad. Thus, the therapist might point out, "Even though you say I am a terrible therapist, you have started coming to sessions on time."

DEALING WITH THE POSITIVE TRANSFERENCE

The focus of interpretation should be on the primitive, grossly exaggerated idealizations that reflect the splitting of all good from all bad object relations. These must be interpreted systematically as part of the effort to work through the primitive defenses and to integrate self and object representations. The counterpart of primitive idealization is a sense of persecution. In contrast, the less primitively determined, modulated aspects of the positive transference should not be interpreted in the early phase. Respecting these aspects of the transference fosters gradual development of the therapeutic alliance. For example, indications that the patient views the therapist as a helpful, interested person should not be interpreted; but if the patient treats the therapist with gross idealization, then a statement such as, "You treat me as if I can do no wrong" is appropriate and necessary.

EXAMINING THE MEANING OF BEING GIVEN AN INTERPRETATION

In the early phase of treatment, the patient's primitive orientation makes experiencing the process of receiving an interpretation seem more significant than its content. It is important that the therapist be alert to and explore what it means to the patient that an interpretation has been made.

Consistent with the patient's overall primitive, intensely exaggerated orientation during this phase is the tendency to see the therapist's actions as powerful, concrete acts of reward and punishment. Because the therapist's most consistent act is that of making an interpretation, it is seen as the vehicle through which the therapist dispenses magic. Looked at from the point of view of primitive defenses, experiencing the interpretation as a wonderful gift is the expression of idealization, while seeing it as worthless signifies devaluation. In either case, the process of therapy is being attended to at the expense of the content.

These magical aspects must be resolved if the patient is to attain the status of collaborator. For example, one borderline patient was observed to make frequent notations on a pad during his session:

Therapist: I notice that you're making some marks on your pad whenever I speak.

Patient: Yes. I'm counting how many times you talk.

Therapist: Why do you do that?

Patient: It helps me know if you care about me. I count up the number of times you speak, and when I go home I compare that number to the last session. That's how I tell how much you're giving me.

Therapist: Does it matter what I say?

Patient: Not so much. What really counts is how many times you tell me why you think I'm doing what I'm doing. Then I know you're really listening to me and concerned about me.

Therapist: So it's very important that I care about you and you've devised a scheme to answer that question for yourself. Can you see you're also treating what I'm saying as if it were worthless?

Regarding the patient's treating the interpretation as an effort at control, consider the following exchange:

Patient: I purposely wore this short skirt today to be sexy. I knew it would turn you on.

Therapist: And what would happen then?

Patient: Then you couldn't concentrate on your work.

Therapist: Could it be that your being "sexy" in this instance is a way of expressing anger?

Patient: I knew you'd say that. All you want to do is to take away my interest in sex. You want to turn me into some sexless creature.

ASSESSING THE EFFECT OF THE INTERPRETATION

Borderline patients in the initial phase of treatment may be quite suspicious of the therapist and feel they must placate the therapist or ward off his or her efforts by seeming to comply. Thus, after making an interpretation, it is important that the therapist attempt to assess the effect that it has had on the patient. A productive interpretation should produce further spontaneous elaboration on the patient's part.

When this does not occur, as, for example, when the patient blandly appears to agree with the interpretation and then changes the subject, the therapist might say, "Though you say you agree, you don't seem to go further with what we are talking about."

FEELING FREE TO CLARIFY AND CONFRONT

Expressive psychotherapy is frequently misunderstood as requiring the therapist to be passive. Neither activity nor inactivity is desirable per se. Whenever the therapist is uncertain about what the patient is saying, he or she should request further clarification from the patient: "What you're saying isn't clear to me. Could you give me an example?" By requesting clarification when necessary, the therapist indicates that he or she is not omniscient, reestablishes the patient's responsibility for providing data, and helps to maintain the overall inquiring attitude. Thus, the therapist is free to be active when necessary.

If the patient's perception is clearly inaccurate, the therapist should feel free to clarify and confront the patient with the inaccuracy. This is a first step toward efforts at improving reality testing, and it is crucial in setting the stage for interpretation. For example, the patient accuses the therapist, "You just slammed the door." The therapist may insist, "In fact, I shut it rather quietly." As was discussed earlier, only after the patient can agree with the therapist that the door was not slammed can the therapist make some interpretation about why the patient might wish to experience the therapist in this fashion.

BEING FLEXIBLE ABOUT INTERPRETATIONS

Borderline patients, because of their pervasive use of splitting, assume that others are as rigid as they are about seeing things in black-and-white terms. This tendency is enhanced to the extent that they are unable to separate the sense of self from that of the therapist (because of dominant projective identification). Therefore, flexibility serves to differentiate the therapist from the patient. By demonstrating the ability to hold alternative views of the same person or event, the therapist provides the patient with a model for tolerating ambiguity and appreciating complexity. If, for example, a therapist is considering two different explanations for the patient's behavior, the therapist might well present the patient with both and acknowledge his or her uncertainty about which is the more valid interpretation. For example:

"It could be that your reported difficulty getting here was a result of your fear that I would be angry with you, or it might be that something else was so much on your mind that you were preoccupied. I'm not sure, at this point, which is correct, and perhaps we can come to understand why you did this."

Note that the phrasing serves to reinforce the patient's responsibility as being the final validator of any hypothesis the therapist might offer. The therapist also indicates a willingness to change an interpretation based on the patient's subsequent input: "As you're showing me, my original idea no longer seems right. It's more likely, given what you just said, that. . . ."

BLOCKING ACTING OUT IN THE SESSION

There may be occasions in the session when the therapist must curb the patient's behavior before making an interpretation.

Halfway through the session the patient begins yelling obscenities at the therapist while covering his ears. The therapist's first intervention would be: "You must stop yelling before we can continue the session. Your yelling and your covering your ears do not permit you to hear and make it impossible for me to be of any help to you." Once the patient stops this behavior, the therapist needs to interpret the behavior, for example, "You are very angry at me and at the same time wish to put me in a position where I cannot help you, which will justify your becoming even more angry."

AVOIDING TAKING SIDES

The patient frequently attempts to engage the therapist in siding with one aspect of the self against another, and, as integration occurs, in siding against someone else. In either case, the result of the therapist's indulging such efforts would be in violation of the position of technical neutrality. For example, a patient is speaking about her anger at herself for deciding not to go to law school. She exclaims: "It's not normal to be so angry at myself. No normal person would act that way!" Rather than accept her invitation to side with her self-reproaches, the therapist might reply, "Whether that's how a normal person would feel or not, I think we could try to understand your dilemma."

An Illustration of Work in the Early Phase

The following example from the psychotherapy of a thirty-four-year-old borderline man illustrates some of the methods described in the foregoing. Note the sequential shifts from one self-object dyad to another as the therapist interprets the active object relation in the session.

From its inception, the treatment of this patient had been colored by the patient's condemnation of the therapist during sessions, by repeated challenges to his technique, and by personal attacks upon his character. In spite of this manifest attitude, the patient came to every session and maintained the initial treatment contract, although he repeatedly tested its limits. During the session immediately preceding the one examined here, the patient had expressed anger at his mother for not visiting him during his recent brief hospitalization for a medical procedure. This demonstrated, he felt, that his mother really cared nothing for him.

The session began with the patient's insistence that the therapist answer a question that he had raised during the previous session and that had not been answered to his satisfaction. The therapist responded that he had answered the question and wondered why the patient began the session by directing him to talk about a particular topic. The patient answered that he did not know what to say. A series of exchanges followed in which the therapist reminded the patient that the basic instruction was to say whatever came to mind, and the patient continued to insist that he did not know what to say.

After a short time this exchange took on the quality of a tug-of-war. The therapist characterized this aspect of the interchange as a contest to see who was going to make whom talk. He added that he surmised that the patient would experience talking freely to him as a defeat in this contest and would feel humiliated. The patient responded that he did not know the therapist and therefore felt uncomfortable telling him anything. The therapist's effort to explore this feeling was met by additional statements that the patient did not know what to talk about. The standoff continued until the patient finally commented upon the interaction himself: "We're going in circles."

Taking this remark as a clue that he had distanced himself sufficiently from the struggle for the moment to observe the process, the therapist chose to offer his hypothesis: "Yes, and these are circles of a power relation. I think there are two powers struggling here in this room—two persons trying to read each other's minds. The one who manages to read the other person's mind without letting his mind be read is triumphant. The one whose mind is read is defeated, humiliated, mistreated." The patient insisted that the therapist wouldn't have to read his mind if he simply answered his question. The therapist continued, "Everything would be all right if I were not so stubborn and were to obey you." Finally he offered an interpretation of the underlying object relation: "And for all this I'm like a stubborn child rebelling against a dominant, insistent, rigid mother."

For the first time in the session, the patient simply remained silent. After a long pause he resumed by reintroducing his feeling that the therapist seemed like a stranger and asked him another question. A new struggle developed over whether or not the therapist had answered the question. The patient became explicit about the question that he felt was unanswered, and the therapist could agree that he had not answered it. At this moment, the therapist perceived the patient as suddenly amused, apparently trying to hide a smile. He confronted him with this observation.

The patient responded by naively asking why he and the therapist could not just have a normal conversation. Psychotherapy did not follow the conventions of an ordinary conversation, the therapist reminded him. Just as the session was about to end, the patient revealed that he was quite angry that the therapist had not asked about his health in the previous session, his first session back after the brief hospital stay. He continued that this indicated that the therapist did not genuinely care for him. Thus, in the last few minutes of the session, a new self-object dyad emerged in the transference—the sickly child angry at a cold, uncaring mother. Via a circuitous route spanning two sessions, the patient's angry feeling of being unloved by a controlling mother was now transposed to the transference.

This session illustrates how an important self-object relation is avoided by the activation of a different dyad in the transference. The clarification, confrontation, and interpretation of that part object relation led in sequence to overt disagreement, to its intensification, to an uncharacteristic silence, and finally to the emergence of a new self-object experience with the therapist.

CHAPTER 7

The Advanced Phase: Working with Higher Level Defenses and Transferences

In dealing with primitive defenses and transferences (the early phase of the treatment), the important task is to transform the patient's chaotic experiences, behaviors, and interactions in the hour into a dominant primitive object relation. This transformation is, in effect, a translation into a cognitive structure verbalized by the therapist; it takes the form of a hypothetical relationship that includes a combination of the patient's communication of subjective experiences, the actual behavior in the interaction with the therapist, and the therapist's analysis of his or her own countertransference reaction to the object relation activated in the session by the patient.

During the early stage of the treatment the therapist's main tasks regarding the interpretations of the transference are, first, to define the dominant object relation in the transference and, second, to track the enactment of reciprocal roles of this object relation, again and again pointing out to the patient how the same object relation is activated regardless of who plays what role in their interaction.

A new task that heralds the shift into the advanced stage of the treatment is the interpretation of dissociated or split-off primitive object relations that actually belong together in the sense of representing, respectively, the all good and all bad aspects of the relationship of the patient's infantile self with a significant other. Thus, for example, a primitive object relation of a totally persecutory nature between a sadistic, engulfing mother and a frightened daughter may represent the counterpart to a totally idealized relation between an all-gratifying mother and a blissful child. To point out how these two relationships are artificially separated in order to avoid the contamination and potential destruction of the good relation by the bad one becomes a major task in advanced stages of the treatment. In other words, the consequences of pervasive splitting operations or primitive dissociation are now interpretively reversed, as the therapist attempts to help the patient to tolerate ambivalent feelings toward the same object and ambivalent views of the self.

When the tolerance of ambivalence has been achieved, the patient is able to perceive himself or herself as well as the therapist as a more complex human being and a new dimension of depth in the perception of self and others signals the transformation of part into total object relations. By the same token, the need to protect the self from intensely ambivalent relations with significant others by splitting mechanisms, projection, repression, or acting out, decreases. In contrast to the earlier phase of treatment—in which intrapsychic experience has been often expressed in the form of acting out, of behavior instead of subjective awareness, and of distortion of the interpersonal field—now the patient is able to communicate intrapsychic, subjective experience more freely.

Thus, tolerance for self-reflectiveness increases; language begins to replace other behavior for communication of subjective experience; and trust in the maintenance of an overall good relation with the therapist improves. These developments, which usher in the advanced treatment stages, signal an integration of the concepts of self and of significant others—in other words, the consolidation of ego identity and, with it, the overcoming of the psychostructural characteristics of the borderline personality organization.

The following example comes from a relatively advanced stage of therapy with a borderline patient.

Patient: I just saw *Foreign Affairs* on your desk, which proves you read other things besides psychiatry. You can do all that and I barely manage to go from day to day. I just hate you. I've been resentful of all of this, and on top of that you are surrounded by all these secretaries who come rushing in. There is no privacy here. Why can't I see a therapist who has an office in town where it's silent, where there's nobody else around, rather than here with all these mechanical women moving in and out?

Therapist: I have a sense that your anger with me really bridges two contradictory reactions. One, a sense of intense resentment of me as a powerful male whom you hate and envy since you feel that men have it made. This feeling is directly connected to the resentment you have when your boyfriend tries to approach you sexually and you get disgusted with his erect penis. On the other hand, I think you have a completely different kind of emotion in which you feel that you could accept me and tolerate me if you were intimately linked to me in an exclusive woman-to-man relationship, but you feel you don't have a chance with all these secretaries who *really* own me. I think that these two contradictory reactions to me are bridged by rage at me. That rage protects you both from feeling resentful, as you get enraged and try to throw me out of your mind, and from being afraid of all these women who will not tolerate that I exist for you alone in a quiet office in town.

Patient: *(Listening intently and appearing less angry.)* Why do you have to make such long, endless interpretations? I know most of the stuff anyhow. You don't let me express my feelings toward you. You immediately have to link it with other things. You can't tolerate that I should have feelings toward you.

In this episode, the therapist is able to interpret *both* sides of a conflict that for many months had been totally dissociated, that is, the resentment and envy the patient felt toward the therapist as a man with whom she couldn't compete, and the sense of doom she anticipated if she were to be in a good relation with him, in which case mother would "get" her. Her sense of resentment alternated with the fantasy of the therapist as a weak, meek male with a small trunk and penis. At such times she would stare at his crotch. At times she was terrified that she wouldn't be able to see him, and was intensely jealous of his wife and daughter, believing that if his daughter were her own age, he would love her at the patient's expense. These two completely contradictory sets of emotions, each of which was a defense against the other, had to be brought together. The episode just presented occurred when the patient had bridged these two contradictory aspects. She had progressed so that she was aware of the contradictory aspects in her relationship with men, including her attitudes about sex, and could tolerate simultaneously experiencing both rage and longing. In contrast to earlier sessions, in which her fantasy was that a penis was literally formed of shit, and intensely disgusting, she now was able to speak of her resentment and envy of male genitals.

Identifying Entry into the Advanced Phase of Treatment

The advanced phase begins when there is a shift away from the predominant use of primitive defenses (splitting, projective identification, omnipotent control, and so on) toward the use of more advanced defenses (projection, reaction formation, isolation of affect, repression, and so on). Concomitant with the reduction in splitting, the patient gives evidence of better integrated self and object representations— experiencing self and others with greater complexity and continuity, and developing the capacities to bear anxiety and to better control impulses. In other words, there is a higher level of defensive functioning, better integration of ego identity, and less ego weakness.

The following features of the treatment indicate to the therapist that the patient has reached this stage.

1. There is a reduction in the patient's use of action to cope with internal states. Thus, acting out, both within and outside of sessions, decreases and is replaced by increased verbalization. The patient may

describe a desired action instead of doing it. For example, a patient whose treatment had been characterized by prolonged provocative silences might signal the entry into this phase by speaking of, rather than acting upon, the wish to remain silent.

2. The patient demonstrates an increased capacity for anticipation, becoming able to predict behavior typical of the past. For example, "Here I am talking about my rage at my mother; if I follow my usual pattern, I'll soon feel like attacking someone."

3. The patient will demonstrate evidence of a beginning capacity to internalize the therapist in the sense of fantasizing his or her thoughts and actions more realistically, less often in the earlier primitive, highly idealized or persecutory light. For example, the patient says, "I just caught myself thinking that if I said, 'The world sucks,' you would tell me that I tend to see everything in black-and-white terms."

4. The patient will be more detailed in describing others, the self, and the therapist. In turn, the therapist will find it easier to remember people that the patient is talking about because of their more three-dimensional quality. For example, the patient might say about the therapist: "Though I'm angry with you, I also remember that you never break our appointments. I also remember that by the end of last session, even though I got very upset during the session, I felt safe." In presenting more complex images of self and others, the patient is indicating a coming together of split-off part object representations. The descriptions may appear more complicated but, in fact, they reflect a greater capacity for differentiation. Because of the patient's increased ability to combine disparate images, these new, more integrated, descriptions may paradoxically appear to be more contradictory than previous descriptions. For example, a patient, early in the treatment, described himself as sadistic in a simple way (reflecting features related only to fantasied aspects of one parent) but has come, through increased recognition and integration of the contributions of both parents, to describe himself in a more complexly sadistic fashion. Similarly, a patient had previously described herself as sexually inhibited, and as occasionally attacking her husband verbally in public. Now she describes herself as communicating derogatory behavior toward her husband before opportunities for sexual intimacy, displaying a rigid, disgusted attitude toward his genitals. This inhibits his functioning, but she then wants him to overcome all these obstacles by tender yet controlling behavior. It

is understood that a patient in this later phase may experience himself or herself dystonically as a bundle of contradictions.

5. The relationship with the therapist deepens, with both an appropriate appreciation of the therapist's contributions to the therapy and a more empathic, realistic observation of him or her as a person. Patients may express remorse over previous hostile behavior vis-à-vis the therapist: "Boy, I remember how you just took it for so long." A corollary is that they begin to show the same concern about their own lives, often expressed in terms of their recognition of how they have wasted time both in the therapy and, more generally, throughout the course of their lives: "I screwed up my life and I'm running out of time."

6. Patients will demonstrate an increasing capacity to recall their shared history with the therapist; by contrast, in the previous phase the therapist had to do most of the remembering of what went on between them.

7. Perhaps most important, there is a decrease in abrupt, even violent, transitions from one affective state to another, with the establishment now of continuities that bridge affect states and contradictory relations with the therapist. In other words, mutually contradictory transference dispositions tend to get mixed up and in the process acquire new emotional depth and complexity. A patient stated, for example, that he was afraid that the therapist might be impatient and critical with him, while, at the same time, he was aware that these were his fantasies and that she was, on the contrary, attentive and interested in understanding and helping him.

8. Patients may give evidence of autonomous work in the sessions. For example, they may talk thoughtfully about themselves without requiring the therapist's urging or inquiring, and listen to the therapist's comments without feeling compelled to elicit them impatiently. They are now involved in a collaborative relationship in which they provide material to the therapist, while the therapist's reactions become an important source of information to them.

9. New information may be forthcoming, for example, regarding "secrets" kept from the therapist over an extended period of time. Patients may communicate openly and honestly about areas that previously were too frightening to bring up, and begin to share with the therapist fantasies about him or her—while remaining aware that these are fantasies and that it is not dangerous to share them.

Patients Who Remain in the Stage of Primitive
Defenses and Transferences

There will, of course, be patients for whom the signs of advancement do not appear, even after years of work. The therapist must diagnose the reasons for the chronic lack of change. Although variability in functioning from session to session is expected, a significant lack of progress over a long period is a manifestation of a therapeutic impasse, usually characterized by one or several of the following phenomena.

1. The patient implicitly or explicitly devalues what has happened throughout the therapy, so that after years of treatment the therapist feels as if work is just beginning.

2. Severe acting out does not diminish in response to the therapist's interpretations or to providing structure in the treatment.

3. The patient continually demonstrates through words and deeds being unable to depend on the therapist. The patient may show no guilt about considering dropping the therapist, or in fact doing so. Generally, with such patients, efforts at confrontation produce in the patient a feeling of being attacked.

4. Running through the sessions is a thread of the patient's continual attempt to tease the therapist with promises of success, followed by self-destructive failures and indifference. For example, a patient for years appears to be working toward going through college and seems to be seeking the therapist's collaborative efforts in that goal, then, through sabotage, fails to graduate and sees in this only a triumph over the therapist.

5. The patient displays sustained dishonesty in sessions despite repeated efforts at interpretation.

6. Severe negative therapeutic reactions are present. That is, there is a clear tendency to worsen at a time when the therapist is experienced as genuinely interested in understanding and helping the patient. *Negative therapeutic reaction,* as will be discussed further in chapter 11, does not refer simply to lack of improvement, but is a definite worsening when help seems to be forthcoming from the therapist. It is often accompanied by an implicit sense of triumph, as if getting worse implied a defeat of the therapist. Milder forms of negative therapeutic reactions, such as worsening in patients with strong depressive personality features as an expression of unconscious guilt, are the counterparts of similar

reactions in borderline patients at advanced stages of treatment, when the tolerance for ambivalence also signals the capacity for experiencing guilt over their aggressive behavior toward the therapist, who is also loved. This negative therapeutic reaction, which reflects the integration of superego functions, however, must be differentiated from severe forms of this reaction, which indicate that the patient has not yet reached the advanced stage of treatment. The dominant aspect of negative therapeutic reaction at a severe level is the presence of conscious or unconscious envy of the therapist as a giving person, and a vengeful effort to spoil whatever the therapist might have to offer.

A particularly severe combination of negative therapeutic reaction, paranoid and sadomasochistic interactions in the transference, destructive or self-destructive behavior, and some degree of dishonesty are presented by patients with *malignant narcissism,* that is, the combination of narcissistic, paranoid, and antisocial tendencies and ego-syntonic sadistic or self-mutilating behaviors (Kernberg 1984). Upon diagnosing such a treatment impasse the therapist should call attention to this serious problem in the treatment and examine the patient's response. Occasionally the discussion will provide clues to an unnoticed transference paradigm that can be interpreted. Sometimes, however, no resolution of such a longstanding impasse will be forthcoming. At such a point in treatment, referring the patient for a consultation is often highly valuable. In a few, very severe cases, the therapist may recommend a change in treatment modality to long-term hospital treatment or even no treatment at this time.

7. Patients who show an incapacity to reach the advanced stage of treatment typically do not learn in the therapy, and their relationship with the therapist does not deepen—the rigid, stereotyped views of the therapist that emerge as part of primitive or split-off transferences remain unchanged.

Treatment Principles

As evidence of increasing integration begins to accumulate, the particular dominant part object relation activated in the transference has to be integrated with other part object relations. In this process, positive and negative aspects of the patient's self-concept are linked and integrated simultaneously with corresponding positive and negative aspects of the patient's object representations.

Following a sequence in which the therapist had been confronting a patient's view that the therapist was intentionally harmful, the therapist (after having established that this was indeed the patient's view of him) said, "So, it could be that you are seeing in me something that is really trying to control you from the inside. To put it differently, it may be that you are struggling with powerful malignant forces in *you* that tend to make you see me as the danger, precisely because I am here to help you; it may be that you are attributing to me that same hostile attitude toward you."

If the patient is able to accept this interpretation, the therapist can go further and state: "Now you can see how, at the time you felt hurt because you believed I was attacking you, you also admired me and felt loving toward me. But because you have these loving feelings, you couldn't acknowledge your anger toward me and had to believe that it was I who was hostile to you. Now you can allow yourself to see that you have both loving and hating feelings toward me and yet we both are still alive and well, and are able to sit in the room together."

In the advanced stages of psychotherapy, content other than the here-and-now becomes appropriate for investigation. Interpretations linking up past with present become important for the first time. Because of the increased integration, the interpretation of dreams may also become useful. In general, in the early stages of treatment, dream analysis should be limited to exploring the conscious, particularly affective content of dreams, linking the corresponding meanings with dominant themes in the transference and other affectively dominant material of the patient's life. At later stages of the treatment, the patient may be encouraged to associate to the manifest content of salient dreams, and emerging unconscious meanings may be integrated into overall interpretations, particularly transference interpretations. In very advanced treatment stages, standard dream interpretation along psychoanalytic lines may become feasible. There, the therapist's experience in dream analysis becomes the limit-setting factor in the utilization of this technique. Our emphasis, however, is on avoiding the danger of premature and isolated efforts at dream analysis in the early stages of therapy with borderline patients.

With the significant resolution of primitive transferences, the activation of early aspects of the self-concept in the transference and of early relations with significant others have a more realistic, differentiated quality that allows the therapist to relate what is now activated in the transference to real persons in the patient's unconscious past. This means that the therapist may now clarify self experiences that are both reflections of the infantile past and sophisticated and complex; the patient's projection onto the therapist of parental images also has a more specific, individualized, complex quality and reveals more realistic features of significant others in the past.

In addition, at this advanced stage of the treatment, it is easier to discern *intersystemic* conflicts, that is, conflicts between an integrated ego or self, on the one hand, and repressed or dissociated, unacceptable impulses (the id) on the other, and between conscious values of the ego and the unconscious infantile morality represented by the superego. Now conflicts are no longer intrasystemic but predominantly intersystemic.

Because the patient now has the capacity to develop a coherent sense of self over time, explorations of the contributions of early history to the present state become meaningful. Genetic interpretations are possible in this phase, and reconstructions may be profitably offered.

The following case illustrates the transformation of primitive into advanced transference dispositions, that is, the activation of transferences within which positive and negative feelings tend to become combined and in which extreme, fantastic images of self and parental figures are shifting into more complex representations of them.

The patient had been oscillating between two alternative relations with the therapist: one in which the therapist was perceived as a warm and receptive, understanding and not controlling parental image—a representation, it turned out, of an ideal mother; and the other, in which he was perceived as a harsh, dominating, but sexually tempting and dangerous father figure. When the therapist simply sat back and listened, the patient saw him as soft, feminine, somewhat depressed, and soothing. But she could not accept any interpretation from him because any interpretive comment transformed him into the aggressive, sexually seductive father, whose interpretive remarks felt to her like attacks.

The therapist pointed to these oscillations and asked the patient how she understood them. She said that when she felt him to be a soothing, feminine, depressed person, she was able to listen to him and feel understood, until he would again "make the mistake" of becoming a masculine and controlling figure!

Over a period of several weeks, the therapist interpreted her double split of him (as masculine and feminine, bad and good) as an effort to avoid the conflict between (a) the need for a good, warm relation with a mother who could understand and give her love—but who also forbade sex with father, and (b) the need to be a receptive feminine woman to a masculine man standing for a father able to "penetrate" her in spite of her acting as if she rejected him (but, by the same token, threatening her relation with mother). The therapist also interpreted her getting stuck in that situation as reflecting a very early relationship with her mother, probably stemming from the second or third year of life, in which she felt that her mother could listen to her only when depressed and listless, while any active interest from her mother seemed like an intolerable controlling dominance. The therapist added that this reflected one more deep reason for her incapacity to shift into a dependent relation with a man who, at the same time, would be sexually attracted to her; not having the security of a basic acceptance and love by a mother who also respected her autonomy, she felt she could not tolerate her sexual feelings toward her father.

Only months later, the therapist was able to point out to her that her perception of her father as a cruel, controlling, and sexually aggressive man represented a condensation of his masculinity with these qualities of dominance displaced from mother onto him. The patient could now integrate these understandings, and the treatment continued to advance in the direction of further work in what turned out to be rather typical oedipal conflicts.

This clinical vignette illustrates how, in an advanced stage of an expressive therapy with a borderline patient (after many months of working through primitive defensive mechanisms and object relations in the transference), a gradual integration of previously dissociated or split-off transference dispositions occurred in the context of a genetic interpretation of the defensive functions of these splits of the transference, and how, as a consequence, changes in the transference developed together with deepening and increased complexity of the object relations activated.

Treatment Strategies and Tactics in the Advanced Phase

The therapist has to continue asking certain questions throughout the treatment. They include the question of whether learning is occurring on the part of the patient, both within and between sessions. The absence of such learning needs to be focused upon as a manifestation of subtle aspects of negative transference acting out, negative therapeutic reaction, or unresolved transference issues in general. The concern about the patient's learning is related to a general attitude on the part of the therapist that may be very helpful, namely, an impatience with impossible situations in each session, matched with an appropriate patience for working through the same issues over an extended period of time.

The diagnosis of therapeutic stalemates requires active work with the corresponding conflicts, be it severe paranoid regressions in the transference, negative therapeutic reactions out of unconscious envy of the therapist, or secondary gain derived from the treatment itself, which in the patient's fantasy replaces life. The therapist needs to raise the question in his or her mind and with the patient of the presence of obstacles to the transfer of the learning in the sessions to other aspects of the patient's life situation. In fact, a growing capacity to become aware of significant parallelism between problems in the transference and problems in other relationships is an indicator that the capacity for integration of contradictory ego states is expanding into the integration of treatment and extratherapeutic experiences and relationships.

The therapist needs to acknowledge as a positive development the patient's increasing tolerance of ambivalence and of the coexistence of healthy and regressive aspects of emotional experiences. Transference regression may now be reduced more quickly by means of interpretation; although repeated regression to early types of primitive transferences may take place, the transformation of these into more integrated, advanced transferences occurs quickly throughout a few sessions or even during the course of the same session.

The following are aspects of the technique of handling material in the advanced stages of the treatment.

1. The interpretations of the transference may be verbalized in ways that rely on an observing part of the patient's ego. In other words, the therapist may take for granted the patient's capacity for self-observation and for quickly grasping additional and related features of a particular issue, rather than having to spell out fully every detail of an observation and to justify the interpretation. A better integrated ego identity permits the patient to maintain both an acting and an observing part of the self, which facilitates therapeutic collaboration. By the same token, there is a stronger alliance between the observing part of the patient's ego and the therapist in his or her role as such. This, the therapeutic alliance, is not to be confused with a positive, dependent transference relationship. The therapeutic alliance is the realistic collaboration of patient and therapist. It increases as a consequence of the analysis of latent and suppressed negative transferences, and with the increasing tolerance of ambivalence.

2. The therapist needs to remain alert to areas of dissociation that may now occur, in contrast to earlier, more primitive types of splitting. The patient may isolate broad areas of intrapsychic experience or external reality as part of an effort to develop compromise solutions between improvement in some areas and a freezing of pathological conflicts or behaviors in others. The therapist, therefore, has to be prepared to challenge such dissociated areas more and more vigorously, depending less on the dominant transference material, and expanding the work to bridge new areas of the patient's extratherapeutic relationships.

3. The therapist needs to raise questions regarding the relationship between the increased transfer of learning from the transference into external reality and from external reality into the transference on the one hand, and the therapeutic goals established at the initiation of the treatment on the other, so that a more realistic assessment of goals achieved and of goals still to be worked on may evolve.

4. It is important to evaluate the extent to which the patient is able to work on psychological issues autonomously in the sessions and be-

tween sessions, not maintaining magical assumptions that all progress is due to the therapist, and that the therapist rather than the patient's own efforts is the ultimate key to change.

5.   It is important to evaluate changes in the patient's capacity for experiencing normal mourning processes during weekends and extended separations from the therapist. In contrast to the violent paranoid anxieties, massive devaluation, panic, and regression triggered by separations in the early stages of the treatment, the patient should now be able to react with more normal longing, sadness, and the capacity to maintain a good internal image of the therapist even during extended periods of separation. Systematic exploration of the reaction to separations is an important preliminary step to the working through of the termination of the treatment. In this connection, the compromise solution represented by secondary gains of treatment ("Everything will be all right as long as I remain in treatment") may be explored as a regressive fantasy, and its defensive functions may be examined in terms of their transference meanings.

6.   Genetic interpretations, that is, linkages between unconscious meanings in the here-and-now and unconscious meanings in the there-and-then, may in the advanced stage of psychotherapy expand the patient's self-awareness into areas of early pathogenic experiences and origins of pathological behavior patterns. During early stages of the treatment it is important to restrict interpretations to the unconscious meanings in the here-and-now. As mentioned before, premature genetic interpretations may foster regression and transference psychosis. Once the patient has been able to tolerate the understanding of unconscious meanings in the here-and-now, however, curiosity as to the origin of transference distortions may be stimulated, and the patient should be encouraged to explore possible origins of patterns that earlier seemed to be perfectly natural and only now are perceived as problematic. Exploration of the past follows the establishment of insight regarding the unconscious meanings in the here-and-now; reversal of this order, that is, the search for explanations in the past before the unconscious meaning in the here-and-now has been clarified, may lead to sterile intellectualization.

7.   The therapist may now shift his or her way of working with dreams. As mentioned before, in the early stages of the treatment systematic dream analysis is usually contraindicated because the pa-

tient's capacity for exploring unconscious meanings without getting lost in a magical world of fantasy is very limited. The optimal use of dreams in the early stages of treatment is to focus on the affectively dominant, conscious elements of the dream content, and to attempt to link that content with other aspects of the transference or of the patient's immediate life. Later the patient may learn to associate to the manifest content of dreams and recover latent aspects of their meaning. In any case, the analysis of dreams is only one aspect among others of the material presented by the patient, and should not acquire magical significance at any point.

8. Countertransference reactions of the therapist may still be intense at this stage, particularly because expressive psychotherapy of borderline personality disorder reaches an advanced stage of treatment through the development of an intense, highly meaningful relationship, including an emotional investment on the part of the therapist that makes the patient an important object in the therapist's fantasy life. Such countertransference reactions, however, are typically briefer, less diffuse, and not overwhelming at this point, and they may lend themselves more easily to be explored within the psychotherapist as information to be translated immediately into part of the material for transference interpretation.

9. All the previously mentioned strategic and tactical aspects of technique in the advanced phases of the psychotherapy should bring about the patient's concern over the termination of treatment, the expectations of goals to be achieved before termination, and the analysis of unrealistic expectations on the part of the patient. What the therapist should expect, and the patient should gradually come to understand, is that the objective of the treatment is to bring about not perfection but an adequate resolution of the structural distortions of identity diffusion, primitive object relations, and defenses, and thus make possible improved life experience and deeper relations with others, and tolerance of conflicts and normal anxiety and depression without decompensation. The fantasies that treatment should go on forever, or that time does not pass during psychotherapy, or that the patient is the only or preferred patient of the therapist are typical resistances in advanced stages of the treatment that require working through in order to facilitate acceptance of termination.

The gradual development of more mature identifications with the therapist should also bring about an identification with the therapist's capacity to be an autonomous human being who tolerates aloneness and loneliness. The gradual working through of both paranoid termination fantasies ("My therapist wants to end the treatment because he wants to get rid of me") and depressive fantasies about termination ("My therapist is ending the treatment because I have disappointed her and I don't deserve continuing the relationship with her") need to be worked through in similar ways in any intensive, long-term psychotherapy.

Here, however, the mourning process is complicated by the reality that very often the therapeutic relationship of the borderline patient within this psychotherapy may objectively have been a better relationship than the patient ever had before; therefore, the loss of the therapist is in reality that of an essential good object. The acceptance of this loss is the counterpart of the patient's needs to work through the awareness of the limitations experienced in the past, to accept the realistic (in contrast to the fantastically distorted) limitations of the parents, and to learn that the psychotherapeutic work is a new ego capacity that, ideally, will help the patient to weather storms after the end of the treatment.

CHAPTER 8

<hr/>

Separation: Interruptions and Termination

Theoretical Considerations

All separations—short or long absences, as well as termination of treatment—can be understood in the light of the psychology of normal and pathological mourning. What comes to mind naturally is that these separations should be understood in terms of separation anxiety. Although borderline patients do react to separations with intense anxiety and symptomatic worsening, so that the term *separation anxiety* seems very descriptive, at a deeper level the reaction is a specific form of pathological mourning. The issue of normal and pathological mourning lends a theoretical basis for the technical approach to separation anxiety in borderline patients.

There is a tendency in the literature to relate the anxiety of the borderline patient directly to the anxiety over missing mother throughout the entire period of separation-individuation, particularly the rapprochement subphase. The relationship is more indirect, however, and the tendency to telescope what is happening now into the first few years of life is a genetic fallacy.

Freud (1917) saw normal mourning as a period of grief or sadness without guilt, a time of working through separation that culminates in the introjection of the lost object. The work of mourning is completed when the lost object has been internalized as an identification of the self with aspects of the lost object. This work is facilitated by the narcissistic gratification of being alive, of still being there, particularly in the case of loss through death or moving away.

Freud (1917) and Karl Abraham (1927) considered pathological mourning as a mourning process that is excessive, cannot be worked through, and is characterized by unconscious guilt over aggression toward the ambivalently loved object. In pathological mourning, there is an attack on the lost and internalized object in the form of an attack on the ego (or the self), motivated by an excessively strict superego. This attack on the internalized, loved and hated object prevents the normal narcissistic gratification of being alive, and the patient is paralyzed in a self-devaluation that originally reflected devaluation of the object yet also serves to expiate guilt.

Because of the complexity of intrapsychic mechanisms involved in the more severe pathology of mourning processes and because Melanie Klein (1948a, 1948b) has focused particularly on this more severe spectrum of pathological mourning, we shall summarize briefly her views about these processes before discussing mourning in borderline patients.*

For Klein, normal mourning also reactivates the guilt and mourning of the depressive position. This guilt is over aggression toward the good internal object, a sense of danger of losing that object as well as the external object currently being mourned. Normal mourning consists in working through the depressive position, reinstating firmly the internal object of early childhood, and internalizing the object that has been lost. The introjection of the external object reinforces the reinstatement of the original good internal object. In addition, the narcissistic gratification of being alive really is a defense against the depressive position in the form of a manic triumph: "I am alive; the other person is dead."

In pathological mourning, Klein goes on, there is a failure in the working through of these processes, caused by an excessive sadism of

*Although such a discussion may seem to be too theoretical and although many of Klein's concepts are controversial, it is important that the reader keep in mind our restricted utilization of her contributions particularly relevant to the subject. Pathological mourning is a pervasive influence on all the relations of borderline patients with significant others. It is not that they are prone to psychotic regressions at times of prolonged separations and terminations, but that key aspects of their pathology of object relations especially emerge at such points and lend themselves to being worked through.

the superego. The superego shows qualities of cruelty, demands for perfection, and hatred of the drives, and this cruelty threatens both the self and the internal object. There is a sense of loss not only of the external object but also of the internal object destroyed by one's own aggression. Now the superego attacks the self, accusing it of having destroyed the internal object. The patient has a sense of internal emptiness and loss not only because of the loss of the external object, but also because of the destruction in fantasy of the internal good object.

So, for Klein, the superego attack is really on the self, not on the internalized object. Suicide, for example, is not really aggression against the external object that has been turned secondarily against the self; it is aggression against the self in expiation for having destroyed the good internal and external objects with the unconscious fantasy that "if I kill myself, only the bad part of me will die, and the good part will survive, together with the good object."

In pathological mourning, the intolerance of the working through of the depressive position may bring about a secondary activation of full-fledged hypomanic defenses in the form of hypomanic denial, experiences of triumph, contempt, omnipotent identification with the lost object, or an identification with the cruel, perfectionistic, hateful superego. Some patients in manic regression treat the available external objects with contempt, a sense of self-righteous superiority, and a tendency toward the *manic feast*—a compulsive introjection, "I don't need anybody; I don't miss anybody; there's plenty of everything I need."

Another secondary defense in pathological mourning is a regression to a predominance of paranoid-schizoid defenses, in which the superego is externalized in the form of paranoid, persecutory part objects. The patient no longer feels depressed, but feels attacked and mistreated. The loss of the external object and the derived loss of the internal object are experienced as the result of an attack by the external object on the self, and full-fledged defenses of projective identification, splitting of idealized and dangerous objects, and efforts to control such dangerous external objects replace the direct manifestations of pathological mourning.

In essence, then, for Klein, the internal mechanisms of pathological mourning are expressed directly in severe depression and indirectly in secondary defenses against depression represented by hypomanic or paranoid-schizoid regressions. These various psychological conditions can be linked to levels of mourning as these are played out in response to separations from the therapist.

Normal mourning is characterized by sadness, absence of self-attack or self-criticism, and mild idealization of the lost object—very much in line with Freud's original description. In neurotic mourning, the sadness is excessive, and there is a tendency to idealize the lost object as a defense against guilt over unconscious aggression toward the object. There is often a clinging dependent reaction to others in an effort to compensate for the loss of the object through closeness to other objects that reassure the individual about his or her own goodness. And there is a tendency toward the expression of guilt in terms of experiences of lack of worth and self-devaluation. This self-devaluation is not delusional; it reflects excessive guilt triggered by the superego's reaction to the loss of the ambivalently loved object.

The mourning processes in borderline patients are characterized by intense anxiety and a fear of doom. Not only does the object seem lost externally, but it is as if the very memory of it has disappeared (reflecting the loss of the internal object as well). There is nothing left except the dread of doom and, very often, a sense of having been unfairly left, dropped, or mistreated by the abandoning object. Here, quite clearly, the mourning process regresses to a paranoid-schizoid constellation. The separation is unconsciously and sometimes consciously experienced as an attack, with rage at the abandoning object. It is this very rage that brings about vengeful wishes toward both the external object and its internal representation as well, with a consequent increase in the sense of emptiness (because of the fantasied destruction of the good internal object), on the one hand, and fear of revenge by the hated object, on the other. This increases even further the fear of being abandoned, the rage because of it, and the destruction of the internal image of the object in a vicious circle in which the patient ends up with an overwhelming experience of fear, emptiness, and of being treated unfairly by fate.

In more severe cases, a generalized fragmentation of emotional experience—a kind of schizoid, withdrawn, and "emptied out" reaction—may develop; it is as if the patient were emotionally dead. Paradoxically, some of these patients may give the surface appearance of being little affected by the separation from the therapist. This may be confused with a devaluation of the therapist, but it really is an extreme, schizoid defense against mourning reactions.

A secondary development that is very common in borderline patients with severely narcissistic features is a response of self-protective devaluation of the lost object. Clinically, the patient appears to have no reaction to the loss of the therapist and during his or her absence acts as if the therapist did not exist. When the therapist returns, the patient acts as if there had been no separation. There is a strange, paradoxical sense of continuity ("as I was telling you in our last session") in spite of a lengthy separation. Other narcissistic mechanisms may be involved, such as devaluation as a defense against envy of the therapist's independent life.

At a still more severe level of reaction to mourning processes, there may be a transitory psychotic decompensation. Here, a defensive refusion of idealized self and object representations takes place, in a defense against acknowledging the reality of separation. Clinically, this may look like a loss of reality testing, diffuse splitting, and fragmentation at a psychotic level.

Therapeutic Principles

The technique for dealing with separation and termination reactions requires diagnosing the level of these processes and helping the patient work them through. That means, first of all, diagnosing the actual level of mourning responses in the patient. A patient should not be offered interpretations about the reactions to the therapist's absence when, in fact, there was no reaction at all!

It is important to monitor the sequence of separation reactions of each patient, which includes what happens over ordinary weekends, longer breaks in therapy, illness of the therapist, vacation time, and, finally, at termination itself. The best way to prepare for termination is to work through the anxieties around separation as they repeat themselves, again and again, and as they gradually change throughout the treatment.

It is important to evaluate the dominant fantasies and object relations behind a patient's statement, such as, "I am depressed," or "I am anxious," or "I am enraged." The patient says: "You're leaving. I am frightened." The therapist should ask: "Frightened about what? What are your fantasies about that?" —"I'm enraged." —"About what? What are your fantasies about that?" In other words, it is crucial to diagnose the full object relation, expressed by the fantasy underlying the patient's reaction about the separation, and to analyze these fantasies and correspondingly activated object relations in terms of the oscillation between depressive and paranoid-schizoid mechanisms and secondary defenses against mourning. In general, there is an advantage in interpreting paranoid before depressive anxieties; this holds particularly true for the analysis of separation reactions.

For example, what are the patient's fantasies about why the therapist is leaving? Is the therapist leaving because of his indifference, his greediness, his wanting to have a great time and not work so hard, his callousness, his secret depreciation of the patient? All of these are typically paranoid fears activated by separation. Or is the therapist leaving because he has become damaged by the patient, or because he is exhausted by the patient's demands? In other words, is it the patient's badness that has driven the therapist away? These are typically depressive fears derived from unconscious guilt of having damaged the good object.

As termination approaches, the patient may express a variety of intense reactions. He or she may interpret the ending as an abandonment, a final expression of the therapist's secret hatred. On the other hand, the patient may reverse the process, feeling that it is he or she who is leaving the therapist. At times, there may be a manic-like glee associated with this reversal—"The end of treatment. What a relief!" Still another response is of a more paranoid nature—the patient fearing that the therapist may "discover" her pleasure at leaving him, and retaliate. Furthermore, termination may be experienced as abandonment because the patient has disappointed the therapist and does not deserve continued treatment. Or the patient feels guilty about looking forward to a happy life while leaving the therapist behind to deal with other impossible people. "Growing up" may unconsciously mean the therapist's death. All of these reactions reflect depressive anxieties connected with termination.

As the patient learns to experience mourning—overcoming paranoid regressions and not moving into the depressive position—he or she begins to accept ambivalent feelings toward the therapist. The goal is to tolerate the ambivalence involved in all human relations; the therapist's work on mourning links up with the interpretation of specific splits between idealized and persecutory object relations from which borderline patients suffer.

From this viewpoint, the integration of contradictory part object relations into total ones is both an analysis of the mourning processes that are caused by this very integration and a preparation for the analysis of mourning processes at termination. Every integration of love and hatred activates guilt and, therefore, remorse over past behavior that cannot be undone. The past becomes a lost opportunity; there is an increased sense of reality and of the passage of time, and a heightened awareness of the finite, transitory nature of all human relations, that is, of death. In this sense, then, integration signifies mourning and preparation for termination. Mourning processes have to be explored and tolerated rather than defensively avoided or eliminated.

It is important to keep in mind that the mourning process will not end with the termination of treatment, but will go on, and the patient should be made aware that there will be a continuation of the process of mourning to be worked through independently. In the therapist's countertransference, termination or extended separations may bring up guilt over mistreating the patient: "How can I do this to the patient, end the treatment?" The patient convinces the therapist that it is really inhuman ever to end treatment. Or the therapist may have to work through his or her own depressive reactions in terms of overconcern for the patient's health or safety, and an unrealistic sense that the patient will not be able to become autonomous or even survive without the therapist. It is important to remember that separations are growth experiences for everybody, including therapists.

Some Practical Arrangements

VACATIONS AND SCHEDULE CHANGES

The therapist should let a patient know in advance of a vacation, ideally by at least three months. Six months' warning is feasible for patients who are advanced in their treatment; but "six months from now" may be meaningless to patients in the middle of intense and chaotic transferences—time is apparently nonexistent to them. Later in the treatment, the therapist's extended vacations may be prepared for over a longer time.

The therapist should be predictable, so that the patient can rely on the stability of the treatment situation. Scheduling sessions at the same hour every day can have a tremendous stabilizing influence. Nevertheless, a therapist who has to change hours frequently or who travels a lot may set up arrangements that are equally satisfactory as long as they remain predictable. For example, a therapist may set up an additional, alternate session each week that is not used normally. A therapist who is often and irregularly absent may go through the monthly schedule at the beginning of each month, telling the patient which of the "switch" hours will be used; this may be a satisfactory arrangement even with psychotic patients.

COVERAGE

Not every borderline patient needs a substitute therapist when the therapist is away on vacation. Such provisions should not be made routinely, only for legitimate reasons. In early stages of the treatment, coverage will be needed more frequently, especially for patients who present severe acting out and for whom external support is inadequate. A patient who reacts to the therapist's absence with severe depressive reactions, suicidal tendencies, or psychotic decompensations may require a supportive structure while the therapist is away.

Most patients, can decide for themselves whether to consult the substitute therapist. The therapist may say: "So-and-so will be available to see you. Feel free to make an appointment or not." With other patients, one may have to insist, "You have to see so-and-so while I am away." In deciding, "Should I make coverage obligatory; should I make it elective; should I not offer it to the patient?" the therapist usually finds an optimal answer by considering the danger of acting out, the likelihood of severe regression, or the possibility that new symptoms will require preventive intervention.

With adequate treatment the patient gradually needs less coverage and makes less use of it. If a patient continues to be in need of coverage over several years, the treatment has problems. In theoretical terms, the patient is probably stuck at a primitive level of intolerance of separation—something is not being worked through.

The covering psychiatrist, with the patient's agreement, should be informed fully about the patient. If the therapist thinks that coverage is indispensable, he or she may decide to provide it even if the patient is opposed to it—then the arrangement becomes part of the total structuring required by the treatment. Obviously, the substitute therapist must be informed about all the issues that may be relevant to potential developments while the therapist is away.

There are two main problems with which a covering therapist has to deal. First is the separation from the therapist: the covering psychiatrist should feel free to discuss fully with the patient the mourning reaction. Second is any immediate life situation that emerges as a true crisis: it is important to explore whether it is truly a crisis or whether it is simply a transference expression, or displacement, as is usually the case with problems that have existed for many months. The borderline patient may attempt to force the substitute therapist to solve a problem immediately, when the patient has not taken the opportunity for months to work on it with the therapist. The substituting therapist must not be seduced into engaging in magic—feeling the need to provide immediate improvement or help to patients who have long-standing, unresolved problems.

The substitute therapist should also interpret freely the patient's efforts to split the two therapists. The patient may say: "Oh, I'm so glad to see you. You're so wonderful. You are warm and nice, I wish my therapist were like you." Or the patient may say: "What do you know? You are just a beginner! I can see from your office that you are very insecure. The greatest therapist around has just left me. How can *you* help me?" Understanding the splitting process helps to protect the substitute therapist from the intense ambivalence triggered at this time. It is advantageous for the substitute therapist to avoid introducing new techniques or new information. The patient may try to seduce the covering therapist: "Do you think it is all right if I now go to Alcoholics Anonymous meetings?" or, "Is it helpful that I use acupuncture?" The substitute therapist should maintain the prior structure in the absence of unexpected developments outside the range of communications with the therapist.

TRANSFER

Transfer to another therapist should be prepared over time. One should permit the patient a preliminary visit with the new therapist, but there should not be an overlap of the two treatments. A patient has the right to reject a recommended therapist, and should then be referred to somebody else. If the patient says, "Oh, this one is even worse," the therapist should think seriously whether to transfer the patient to anybody or whether to tell the patient: "I have suggested two people. You may select one of the two, or else you will have to make a search independently for someone with whom you can work."

As always, it is important to work through the mourning process, and, of course, to remind oneself that much of this working through will have to be carried out with the new therapist. The new therapist may be either idealized or depreciated, and will need to be prepared for this.

A crucial issue is that the therapist who accepts the transferred borderline patient should not take for granted all the information and all the treatment structure he or she has inherited. One must reevaluate from the beginning the diagnosis, treatment indications, techniques, structure, and other arrangements. For example, the new therapist has to ask: "Does this patient really need medication?" "Does this patient really need an auxiliary therapist?" "Are there obscure areas that have never been clarified?" "Am I inheriting a myth that has been established in the previous treatment, for which I have no evidence, and that should not be taken at face value?" "What are the treatment goals now?" "What are the patient's life goals, and how have they changed?" That is, the new therapist has to reevaluate the treatment and to have full freedom of decision making.

The departing therapist should protect the freedom of the new therapist, and remember not to ask anybody to give more love to a third person than comes naturally. It is highly inappropriate for the departing therapist to tell the new therapist something like: "Look, this interesting patient needs somebody like you. Only you can help the patient, who needs to be given very much love because of being so deprived." The departing therapist must avoid unloading onto somebody else his or her guilt for leaving the patient.

TERMINATION

Treatment should be terminated when there has been (1) adequate symptom resolution and (2) significant personality change so that identity diffusion has been resolved, ego strength has been increased, and initial treatment goals have been reached. In the process, some of the patient's life goals will have been approached as well. Yet when a patient is treated successfully over a period of years, the goals may expand to the verge of extending the treatment endlessly, with both patient and therapist holding an unconscious fantasy that this patient should become no less than a perfect person.

Realistically, one should assess whether the treatment has reached a point of diminishing returns. Sometimes the assessment has to be related to external circumstances, the opportunities a patient may have in work or marriage, and the residual incapacities in the patient's personality resources—for example, limited intellectual resources, which may limit a patient in a profession, or severe, intractable sexual inhibitions. Borderline patients with sexual promiscuity and apparent freedom to enjoy polymorphous infantile sexual trends may become temporarily inhibited in advanced stages of their treatment as oedipal conflicts are activated at higher levels. Borderline patients with initially severe sexual inhibitions may develop almost intractable, chronic sexual inhibitions in spite of, or because of, greater personality integration; for these patients adjunctive sex therapy—by a different therapist—may occasionally be considered in the advanced stages of treatment.

There may have been traumatic life developments during the treatment—illness, death, financial problems, or opportunities missed. The patient's adjustment to the reality of life includes developing a realistic awareness of the limits of what can be achieved.

Before setting a date for termination, it is important to differentiate extended stalemates from the conclusion that maximum benefits have been achieved. Because superego functions consolidate in advanced stages of the treatment, severe negative therapeutic reactions may evolve out of an unconscious sense of guilt. These may last for up to a year; the patient gets nowhere and remains clearly in an oppositional or hostile relation to the therapist. The therapist may be tempted to think, "Well, if this patient thinks that I am the worst therapist in the world, and the treatment is not going anywhere, why shouldn't someone else take on this case?" It is important to recognize these late, extended negative therapeutic reactions. Very often the patient has significantly improved in many aspects of life while the treatment is transformed into an ongoing struggle, marked by accusations that the therapist is not helping and not understanding what is going on now that the patient is better. An evaluation of the transference and an assessment of change should help to clarify and overcome this development.

Another danger is that of getting used to transference developments in cases where "nothing seems to happen anymore." There may be an advantage in stepping back and thinking about the patient outside the sessions, or in asking for a consultation, not because of any acute problem but because of a strange, long-term stabilization of the treatment. Sometimes a consultation may open new vistas regarding the total treatment situation. An unconscious dependency on the patient may have developed, in which the therapist who invested many years of effort may experience the end of a successful treatment as a narcissistic injury.

There are certain characterological, long-term defenses against separation that patients may set up early in treatment. For example, a patient may start out the treatment with fears about the end of it, that is, a projection into the future of an immediate fear of abandonment. Behind this fear there may be complex transference developments. For example, secondary gain of treatment may reflect efforts to use the treatment as a replacement for life or as a defense against full engagement in life tasks. For example, a patient may think: "OK, I'll get married. I won't have a good husband or a good marriage, but I have my therapist for the rest of my life." Therapy is used here to avoid a full commitment to other relations. If there has been no progress over an extended period of time, and if the stalemate cannot be explained as a negative therapeutic reaction, but the patient nevertheless is reluctant to end the treatment, the secondary gains of the treatment must be analyzed. This analysis should always be carried out first by the therapist outside the sessions because it should not be dependent on moment-to-moment shifts in transference and counter-transference.

If the treatment of the advanced phase has been successful, its termination should closely resemble that of work with neurotic patients. There is often an initial return of presenting symptoms with familiar self-destructive behaviors or an attack on the therapist or the therapy. If the therapist has correctly assessed the patient's progress to the termination phase, then these destructive efforts should be amenable to interpretation without the reintroduction of parameters.

An essential task of this phase is the exploration and resolution of patients' magical fantasies about the therapist. This is necessary for two reasons: to enable patients to appreciate their own collaboration in the treatment and to reduce the sense of the omnipotent therapist so that a real separation can take place. To the extent that patients cling to their belief in the magical, omniscient therapist, they believe themselves to be always in touch with the therapist and never fully on their own or appreciative of their own efforts.

Patients should be able to talk realistically about future plans; they should show some behavioral evidence that they can at least begin to carry out these plans; and they should be able to acknowledge the meaning of the therapist and of the therapy. It is important to explore not only what has been attained but also the discrepancy between what the patient had hoped for and what has actually been accomplished. Termination should not be dealt with as a trial departure to see how the patient fares; rather, both patient and therapist need to agree that, barring unforeseen circumstances, their work is coming to an end. Evidence of the patient's experiencing a sense of loss will confirm this point. Patients who express excessive gratitude toward the therapist without acknowledging their own contribution may be signalling their difficulty with separation; that possibility should be explored. That does not mean, however, that the therapist should fail to acknowledge the realistic evaluation of his or her own work as well as the patient's contribution to their final product.

The termination of extended treatment should be agreed upon at least six months ahead, to provide time for the working through of the corresponding mourning process. It is important to observe the reactions of the patient from the very moment a date of termination has been set. It is helpful not to taper off the treatment at the end.

Tapering off creates the illusion that the depression will be worked through before total separation. On the contrary, tapering off reduces work with mourning reactions and the meaning of termination.

A solid separation must be maintained through a posttermination phase. The patient may ask, "Can I call you if I have any problem?" The therapist may reply: "Yes, if there's any severe problem, you may call me. But only if there is a severe problem. Otherwise, it is advantageous that you be on your own for at least six months, perhaps a year; and then, if you wish, you can call me and we can evaluate the situation again."

PART THREE

COMMON
COMPLICATIONS

CHAPTER 9

Immediate Threats to the Treatment

Suicide Threats and Suicidal Behavior

Because suicide threats and suicidal behavior frequently present themselves with borderline patients, the therapist should evaluate their likelihood before starting treatment. If suicide is a present or an imminent issue, before beginning the treatment the therapist should clearly delineate for the patient how suicide threats or attempts will be handled. The limits of the therapist's responsibility, the extent of the responsibility of the patient, and possibly the role of the patient's family should be discussed. The initial contract should clearly specify the commitment being asked of the patient by the therapist, as well as what the therapist accepts as a commitment. If in the course of treatment suicide becomes an unanticipated issue, the treatment contract must be renegotiated to include the arrangements under which treatment can continue in the least disruptive way.

If the therapist is convinced, on the basis of solid evidence either in the patient's history or in their present interactions, that the patient is communicating honestly, the therapist will probably be able to trust his or her estimation of the patient's suicide potential from day to day. The major question is not whether the patient is able to trust the therapist but whether the patient is willing and able to communicate honestly.

Certain broad guidelines can be offered for the decision-making process in the evaluation and management of suicide threats and suicidal behavior.

Diagnosis takes into account the intensity of suicidal ideation, plans for action and the accompanying affect, as well as the extent to which depression affects behavior, mood, and ideation. The severity of the depression can be gauged by the degree to which behavior and ideation are slowed down (and concentration thus affected) and sadness is replaced by an empty, frozen mood with a subjective sense of depersonalization. In addition, the presence or absence of biological symptoms of depression (reflected in eating and sleeping patterns, weight, digestive functions, daily rhythm of depressive affect, menstrual patterns, sexual desire, and muscle tone) supplies crucial information regarding the severity of the depression. In general, the more severe the clinical depression accompanying suicidal ideation and intention, the more acute the danger. The sense that there is no alternative is an especially ominous sign.

Impotent rage—particularly when coupled with a fantasy that one's death will make the significant object either recognize one's worth or be crushed by guilt feelings—is another diagnostic indicator of potential suicide. As early as the preliminary sessions, a transference paradigm may emerge in which the patient indicates a belief that the therapist can be affected only through the patient's destruction.

Patients in states of severe depression vary in their ability to control the urge to act on the suicidal impulse. The therapist's judgment on this question is based upon the quality of the relationship with the patient, and on whether impulsive, antisocial, dishonest, paranoid, schizoid-aloof, or psychotic aspects make the patient's verbal commitments unreliable. In addition, the patient's alcohol and drug history will be highly relevant in judging whether promises can be relied upon.

When the therapist feels assured that the patient's word can be accepted, no specific action need be taken so long as the patient is committed not to act on suicidal impulses and continues to be able and willing to discuss thoughts and feelings openly. (Patients who lose this rapport, become too depressed to communicate, or begin to make preparations for suicide must be protected.) Patients may feel relieved by the therapist's alertness to their cues, and hence may become less endangered by suicidal impulses.

When the therapist does not have sufficient confidence in the patient's assurances, he or she must take responsible action, with or without the patient's approval. In such cases, and depending on whether the patient's suicidality is linked to depression or not, the therapist may insist that the patient begin a course of antidepressant medication or electroconvulsive therapy (ECT) and/or be hospitalized. Relatives must be notified of the dangers involved.

Similar protective action must be taken when the patient is either unwilling or unable to give verbal assurances of being able to control the urge toward suicide. The therapist's ultimatum may be that the patient go into the hospital or accept appropriate guardianship. Such actions are necessary even if they lead to a temporary or final disruption of the treatment with the particular therapist.

If convinced that the patient is not severely depressed, the therapist must attempt to evaluate the meaning of the suicide threats and suicidal behavior. It may be revealed that they represent the borderline way of life in which the gestures are an attempt to dominate, manipulate, or control the environment. Frequently, these are the cases of suicidal trends without depression or *parasuicide*. Without a past history of this and with no indication of clinical depression, however, such threats should call attention to transferential issues, which tend increasingly to replace other environmental precipitants as therapy progresses.

If the threats represent attempts to dominate, control, or manipulate others, the therapist must attempt to neutralize the weapon that the threats represent by structuring the relationship to decrease or eliminate the secondary gain involved. For example, suicide threats or suicidal actions should not be rewarded by extending sessions or adding appointments. Examination frequently reveals that these gestures are designed to establish or reestablish control over the environment by evoking anxiety and guilt feelings in others. As treatment continues, the most likely target for control is the therapist.

When the threats represent transference issues, the therapist's goal is to recognize them, ultimately discerning the pattern that leads to the predictability of the impulse.

Active measures to increase the structure help the therapist feel more comfortable and hence more capable of managing the powerful feelings evoked by suicidal patients. The therapist who allows himself or herself to be pressed beyond the limit (as, for example, when an idealizing patient evokes an omnipotent countertransference reaction) typically withdraws emotionally in self-defense, an action that is far more damaging to the treatment than is the firm setting of a structure.

The therapist's most helpful response may be to instruct the patient to go to the emergency service of a hospital for evaluation. By placing the evaluation of suicide in the hands of others, the therapist deprives the patient of the gratification of calling on him or her during suicide episodes, and may prevent the expectation that suicide threats will increase the attentiveness of the therapist by creating the rationale for additional appointments or prolonged telephone conversations. The emergency room physician may recommend hospitalization. If the patient is not willing to follow that recommendation, the therapist should tell the patient and the family that he or she will take no further responsibility for the patient, while offering the names of professionals who the patient and family may choose to utilize. In taking such a position, the therapist should refer back to the original contract, pointing out that it is the patient (or the family) who is choosing not to continue. "We had discussed that your daughter, given her history, might make a suicide attempt while seeing me, as she had done with several of her previous doctors. I told you that, if that were to happen, she would need to go to a hospital to determine whether an inpatient stay was indicated. I also said that I would abide by the evaluating doctor's decision and would not see her until she was discharged. Now, by insisting that I continue to treat her as an outpatient despite my recommendation that she be hospitalized, you leave me no choice but to discontinue the treatment."

The unpredictability of borderline patients' behavior often means that the threat of suicide is switched on and off unexpectedly, an aspect of the problem that must be discussed openly with both the patient and the family. Continued monitoring of suicide potential is necessary, particularly with borderline patients who are vulnerable to a bona fide affective disturbance that may increase the danger of suicide in the course of treatment.

When chronic threats of suicide become incorporated into the patient's way of life, the therapist should tell the family that the patient is chronically apt to commit suicide, indicating to them that the patient suffers from a psychological illness with a definite risk of mortality. The therapist should express to those concerned the willingness to engage in a therapeutic effort to help the patient overcome the illness, but should neither give firm assurance of success nor guarantee protection from suicide over the long period of treatment. This realistic circumscription of the treatment may be the most effective way to protect the therapeutic relationship from the destructive involvements of family members and from the patient's efforts to control the therapy by inducing in the therapist a countertransference characterized by guilt feelings and paranoid fears regarding third parties.

It is important for patients to learn that their threat of suicide has no inordinate power over the therapist; that although he or she would feel sad if the patient died, the therapist would not feel responsible and his or her life would not be significantly altered by such an event.

It is important for the therapist who treats chronically suicidal borderline outpatients to refuse treatment arrangements that require unusual efforts or heroic measures. The temptation to provide heroic treatment provides a clue to the beginning of countertransference difficulties. Whenever more is accepted by the therapist than would be reasonable in the average therapeutic treatment, the end result is a reinforcement of the patient's self-destructive potential, as well as an increase in the likelihood of unmanageable countertransference developments as the therapist becomes exhausted and harassed. The therapist should keep in mind what the "good enough" therapist would be likely to do, and, if there is an inner compulsion to go beyond that, examine his or her motives.

The therapist's acceptance of the possibility of failing with a patient is a crucial element in the treatment of patients with severe suicide potential. The patient's unconscious or conscious fantasy that the therapist desperately wants the patient to stay alive, and that the patient therefore has power over the therapist, needs to be explored and resolved in the treatment.

Every attempted or completed suicide involves the activation of intense aggression not only within the patient but within the immediate interpersonal field. The therapist who seems to react only with sorrow and concern for the suicidal patient is denying his or her counteraggression and buying into the patient's dynamic. Openness to countertransference feelings will enable the therapist to empathize with the patient's suicide temptations, with the longing for peace, with the excitement of self-directed aggression, with the pleasure in taking revenge against significant others, with the wish to escape from guilt, and with the exhilarating sense of power involved in suicidal urges. Only that kind of empathy on the part of the therapist may permit the patient to explore these issues openly in the treatment. With patients who present chronic suicidal or self-mutilating potential, that potential must be explored consistently and woven into the analysis of all interactions with the therapist. Thus, for example, the chronically suicidal patient's destruction of time during the session by remaining rigidly silent may be interpreted as an effort to destroy the treatment and with it any hope of recovery; the in-session interaction with the therapist is, then, a suicide equivalent. This is interpreted to the patient and analyzed.

The patient with severe suicidal potential referred to in the example of a first session in chapter 3 illustrates the therapeutic approach to the danger of suicide. As figure 9.1 illustrates, evaluating the context in which the suicidal threat arises is the crucial first step in managing self-destructive thoughts and actions.

Threats to Quit the Treatment

Patients drop out of treatment for many reasons, some of which are particularly characteristic of borderline patients. Threats to quit the treatment, whether overt or merely implicit, take priority over all other issues except imminent threats to the patient's life or to other people's lives.

The following are among the motives that may prompt a borderline patient either to threaten to drop out of treatment or to behave so as to imply such a threat.

1. The negative transference brings on a threat. Transference is usually conceptualized as the transfer of love or hatred from its original object onto the therapist. The negative transference of borderline patients often includes efforts to rid themselves of hated aspects of their internalized representations of themselves and their objects by projection of these aspects onto the therapist. The patients then seek to

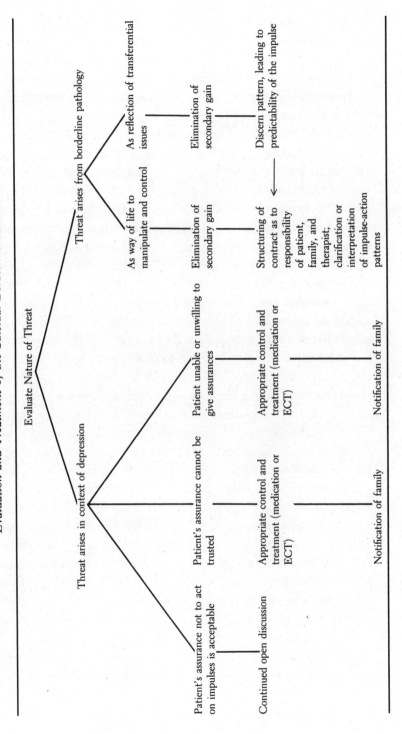

FIGURE 9.1

Evaluation and Treatment of the Suicidal Borderline Patient

control the feared and hated other, perceived now as threatening, incompetent, dishonest, uncaring, or otherwise untrustworthy. Such negative transferences may be manifest in overt accusations, in impulsive abandonment of treatment, or in threats to abandon treatment. Negative feelings may remain outside the patient's awareness and be expressed behaviorally by tardiness, missed sessions, or by withholding information. Patients' complaints of vague fears or uneasiness in the session may also be symptomatic of negative transference.

2. Narcissistic issues often lead to threats to quit the treatment. Close contact with the therapist stirs feelings of envy, jealousy, and competitiveness that to borderline patients feel like assaults upon self-esteem, though it may not be clear that the attack comes from within. Rather, patients may feel that the therapist is actively engaged in trying to humiliate them. They may envy the therapist's ability to help because they feel incompetent to be useful or valuable to anybody else. They may envy the therapist's capacity to experience genuine feelings, while judging their own feelings to be unstable and shallow. Patients may feel competitive with the therapist, so that a success on the therapist's part feels like a defeat for them. This kind of competitiveness, when pervasive and intense, can be a major problem: the therapist's correct understanding of them seems like a success or triumph for the therapist and therefore makes the patient feel even more stupid and inadequate by comparison. Patients may be excessively jealous of the therapist's other patients or inordinately resentful of his or her other interests, feeling that there is no room for them. Their efforts to restore or protect vulnerable self-esteem may include revenge for felt humiliations, or punishment for frustrations felt as both intolerable and unjust.

3. Dependency needs may give rise to threats to quit, designed (consciously or unconsciously) to elicit increased concern from the therapist. If that desired effect is achieved, the patient is motivated to continue making such threats by the secondary gain accruing from the therapist's response. Conversely, the disavowal of dependency needs may take the form of a flight into health heralded by a pronouncement of a decision to end the treatment.

4. Hypomanic states as a defense against depression may lead to an abrupt conviction that treatment is no longer needed.

5. The wish to protect or humiliate the therapist may take the form of threats to quit the treatment when the patient senses countertrans-

ference difficulties expressed in the therapist's fatigue, inattention, exasperation, or feelings of incompetence. The patient may be unable to articulate the sense of being too much for the therapist, simply saying that it is time to end the treatment.

6. Actual demands of family members may lead to threats to quit, when the family experiences the patient's treatment as altering long-standing patterns needed for the psychological homeostasis of the family.

7. Injunctions of internalized representations of the parents stir impulses to quit when the patient experiences attachment to the therapist as being profoundly disloyal to the parents of childhood. One patient, while making some vaguely critical comment about how her parents had dealt with her in childhood, would look up as if expecting a thunderbolt from heaven. Emotionally, it was exceedingly hazardous to utter such a critical comment.

8. When a borderline patient experiences himself or herself as victim and the therapist as persecutor, the patient may sadistically reverse roles and act the part of the one who rejects and abandons the helpless other.

9. Fears of abandonment may lead the patient to leave in anticipation of being left.

10. Guilt or shame over sadistic or sexual wishes toward the therapist or toward other people may lead to an impulse to quit treatment rather than express such fantasies and risk being regarded judgmentally by the therapist. Patients who feel guilty over their dependent longings may regard treatment as self-indulgence and threaten to quit so as to avoid such guilt.

11. Subtle or overt threats to discontinue therapy may reflect an intensification of the treatment rather than its imminent failure. The threat to quit may indicate that the treatment is moving too rapidly or becoming more intense than the patient can tolerate. Such threats may become realities unless dealt with preventively.

The earliest hints about dropping out should be examined and actively addressed. Requests for a reduction in frequency of sessions, talk of plans to move to another geographic area, planning activities that compete for the session times may all be early warning signs of a plan to end the treatment. Alertness to early signs is particularly important when working with patients who have dropped out of previous treatments, because they can be expected to repeat this pattern in the current treatment as well. A patient said, "I have had fourteen other therapists; now I have finally found you. You're perfect." In the following session she announced her intention to terminate the treatment.

A careful, detailed, and technically neutral approach to setting up the treatment contract is the most efficient way of preventing premature dropout. The therapist should systematically explore all the potential reasons for which the patient may not be able to make a commitment to treatment or, once committed, still be at high risk for premature interruption of it (see chapter 3).

In establishing the initial contract, the therapist should forewarn the patient of the wish to quit: "As you continue to experience the suffering that brought you into therapy, you are likely to become discouraged. You may well begin to feel you have gotten the wrong therapist or the wrong treatment, and will be tempted to leave. In this way you could prevent us from understanding what your painful experience is all about." Having warned the patient of this eventuality, the therapist can refer to the prediction later.

During the subsequent course of treatment, the therapist must remain alert to signs of the patient's wish to quit and deal with them promptly. Such signs include canceling or failing to attend sessions, coming late, becoming drowsy or silent, or complaining of not making progress. These behaviors should be addressed actively, the patient being asked to clarify the thoughts and feelings associated with them. If such clarification is not forthcoming, the therapist can offer the hypothesis that the patient is in fact considering quitting and behaving in such a way as to bring the treatment to a halt. Having conveyed to or agreed with the patient that quitting is an issue, the therapist should seek clarification of the patient's fantasies about the impact quitting will have. Such fantasies can be interpreted in the light of the part self–object dyad prevailing in the therapy at this point. "Could it be that you are planning to leave me because today you experience me as abandoning you, leaving you no recourse but to leave first to avoid the pain? Recall that yesterday you saw yourself as controlling me and were afraid that I needed you to stay to preserve my reputation."

Meanwhile, remaining alert to his or her own emotional response to being left, a therapist should assure the borderline patient: "I will not be damaged by your quitting, but I hope we will be able to continue to try to work out our difficulties." Because everyone reacts emotionally to the experience of being left and of failing, a therapist must manage countertransference responses before being able to say truthfully that the patient's quitting is not going to hurt.

Next the therapist interprets the reasons the patient wants to quit, what the patient currently fears, and what the patient hopes to achieve by quitting. One may refer at this point to the initial contract, recalling that patient and therapist had anticipated from the outset that the wish to quit would surface from time to time, and inviting the patient to try to figure out why it is surfacing right now.

The patient may deny the intention to quit, insisting instead that the therapist must hate and want to get rid of him or her. The therapist must first interpret the projection, then elicit the fantasy about the therapist's attitude toward the wish to quit, and finally reiterate his or her actual attitude. If the threat to quit is part of a flight into health or of a hypomanic episode, the therapist should interpret this, calling attention to the distortions of reality involved in the patient's perception of having suddenly overcome all the difficulties.

If the patient and therapist can agree upon the motives prompting the wish to quit, the interpretive process then moves along. If they disagree (for example, the therapist sees the patient as fearful of the changes experienced in treatment, while the patient maintains that the therapist is unconsciously malevolent), an impasse has occurred. The therapist must convey acceptance of the possibility that the patient is going to quit, and clarify his or her reactions to this eventuality. The therapist must accept the patient's autonomy and the inability to control the patient or to understand all of the feelings and motives involved in the wish to leave.

It is not unusual for borderline patients to indicate their intention to quit the treatment in the form of an abrupt pronouncement. Such pronouncements often occur in the session following an interruption of the therapy. "I have decided while you were away that I didn't need you after all." Whether these pronouncements occur in the midst of a session or by telephone, they have a way by taking one by surprise, sounding final and very threatening. Because they mobilize a therapist's anxieties about abandonment and failure, they call for a response that is often difficult to muster, particularly on the telephone. When a patient telephones to say, "I am not coming to tomorrow's session; in fact, I have decided to quit," the therapist might respond to the quality of the pronouncement rather than to the threat itself: "You present your intention to leave as a final decision rather than as something we can talk about. Maybe you have made a final decision, but even so it would be worthwhile for us to discuss it. I am going to be here tomorrow and I hope to see you also."

Because borderline patients experience strong needs to maintain relationships alongside the angers, fears, and projections impelling them to flee threatening attachments, the patient is likely to accept the invitation to discuss the threat to leave. If so, it may be possible to clarify the motives for wanting to quit the treatment. The therapist should try to elicit fantasies about the impact of the pronouncement. The patient may hope that the therapist will be shocked, stunned, paralyzed, disappointed, narcissistically wounded, or rendered helpless and lonely. Ventilation of these fantasies may afford some relief of the patient's anxiety, because verbalizing the fantasies is an alternative discharge channel for the wish to act upon them. It will then be possible for the therapist to correct the distortions of reality: "I would like you to be able to pursue your work in therapy, but my feelings are not going to be hurt if you decide to quit." It may then be possible to proceed to interpret the fantasies, helping the patient understand the wish, for example, to inflict upon the therapist the feelings the patient would have were the therapist abruptly to announce the end of the treatment, or the wish to deny feelings of dependency, to enact hateful feelings, or to obey the real or imagined wishes of the family. Repeated threats to quit treatment must be taken up consistently as an expression of the patient's destructiveness toward the treatment through calling the patient's attention to the evidence of the desire to quit, clarification of the motives and fantasies, and interpretation of these.

Lying and the Withholding of Information

Right behind the first order of priority for intervention (imminent threats to the patient's life, to other people's lives, and to the survival of the treatment) comes deceptiveness. Lying is an expression of how the patient experiences the self, others (in particular, the therapist), and the therapy. In the immediate context, patients may lie for several reasons: (1) to avoid confrontations that will result in their having to assume responsibility for their actions; (2) to avoid the therapist's disapproval or retaliation; (3) to exert control over the therapist; or (4) to express superiority over the therapist. In a deeper sense, lying expresses the belief that all human relationships are basically exploitative or persecutory. In fact, psychopathic transferences—consistent dishonesty, deceptiveness, and manipulation—are usually profound and pervasive defenses against an underlying paranoid transference, that is, a profound conviction of the basic hostility of the therapist, as an expression of the primitive aggressive impulses in the transference. Because the success or failure of the therapeutic task depends upon honest communication, lying must be treated as seriously as any effort at self-destruction. The therapist must try to interpret fully the suppression of information.

An example of the mildest form of deception, in which suppression and splitting are used to withhold information from the therapist, follows.

A patient opens the session by first stating that she doesn't know what she wants to talk about and then declares, "There's nothing." *(Three minutes of silence follow.)*

Therapist: It may well be that there was no particular subject that you wanted to bring up from the beginning of this session. We have agreed, however, that if there's no particular problem on your mind, you should talk as freely as you can about what comes to mind. So I think you are either forgetting that or suppressing what is on your mind, rather than sharing it with me.

Patient: *(One minute pause.)* There isn't anything on my mind.

Therapist: *(After twenty seconds.)* I find that hard to believe. It is very difficult not to have anything on one's mind. It is practically impossible. Now, what's on your mind may come in the form of thoughts, or memories, or images, or perceptions of feelings or fantasies or dreams, or whatever, but it's almost impossible not to have anything on your mind. You looked like you were engaged actively in thinking. So you're not telling me what's on your mind and also not telling me the truth about the fact that this is what you're doing. I'm also thinking that there was a friendly smile on your face when I greeted you outside and that a subtle smile emerged again at the beginning of the session—a smile that you tried to suppress immediately. My tentative conclusion is that part of you was pleased to come here and to see me, but a part of you that is trying to destroy your treatment immediately got into the act, forcing you into provocative silence. If I am correct, there is a struggle going on in your mind around your relationship with me.

Interpretive efforts focusing on lying or withholding of information may take weeks or months, particularly in cases with antisocial features. However long it may take, full resolution of the implications of the patient's lying takes precedence over all other material, except life-threatening acting out. If the patient who habitually lies also shows evidence of life-threatening or treatment-threatening acting out, the treatment should start in the hospital so as to provide the protection and accurate reporting that the patient is unable to provide. Patients who lie habitually and give evidence of serious superego deficiencies tend to project their own moral values onto the psychotherapist and to conceive of him or her as being dishonest and corrupt. The interpretive approach to the transference functions of lying includes, therefore, focusing on the patient's projection of dishonesty onto the therapist. "I am not surprised that you feel that I have billed you for a session that you shouldn't be charged for, because throughout our meeting today you've been making up stories instead of telling me what really happened. It's as if you can't imagine a world in which lying and exploitation aren't everyday occurrences."

Full exploration of the transference meanings of lying, as in all interpretive work, proceeds from surface to depth. Transference interpretations will often first focus on lying as an expression of the patient's hostility toward self as well as of hostility and suspiciousness toward the therapist. Deeper interpretations about the patient's despair can be made only after the aggressive and paranoid components are interpreted.

The following examples illustrate a therapist's confrontational or interpretive comments in circumstances where lying serves different principal functions.

- Lying as an expression of hostility toward the self: "You continuously change your story about what happened. This makes it impossible for me to help you and thus ends up defeating you."
- Lying as an attack on the therapist: "You continue to tell me the same thing even after we have agreed that this is a made-up tale. You treat me, therefore, as if I'm not worthy of your respect."
- Lying as an expression of fear of retaliation: "You seem to fear telling me the truth about having taken my magazine from the waiting room because you think that if you told me, I would become angry and stop seeing you."
- Lying as an expression of disillusionment: "You act as if the only way you can save your skin is to create a fiction about what's happening. That means to me that you have no belief that were I really to know you, anything good could come of it."

Some borderline paranoid patients acknowledge conscious withholding of material in response to paranoid fantasies about the therapist. Whenever manifest paranoid ideation becomes predominant in the early hours of treatment, it is important for the therapist to evaluate carefully whether the patient in fact suffers from a paranoid psychosis. For example, one patient refused to give his real name over a period of several weeks. It was only after considerable exploration of what he thought the therapist would do with the information that he revealed his belief that the therapist would blackmail him. Only repeated efforts at ventilating these paranoid fears and confronting the patient realistically with the absurdity of his fear permitted the reinstatement of his reality testing, and thus, allowed the therapist to begin to interpret the meaning of the transference reactions.

Situations arise in which the therapist has the vague sense that the patient is being dishonest without being able to pinpoint the basis for this impression. In such an instance, it is perfectly appropriate to tell the patient: "I have a sense that you're not being straight with me. Let's explore whether this is my problem or yours." As long as the therapist senses that the patient may be suppressing information, examination of that subject constitutes the highest priority.

CHAPTER 10

Acting Out and Indications for Deviating from Technical Neutrality

Acting Out

The next priority for interpretive intervention, after life- or treatment-threatening behavior and dishonesty or other contract breaches, is that of acting out. Acting out is the expression of an unconscious conflict in the transference in action rather than in emotional experiencing, remembering, and verbal communication. Acting out may provide fundamental information about the patient's conflicts; but by the same token, it prevents insight or personality change by its defensive functions. Because it is highly gratifying, acting out tends to perpetuate itself.

Acting out should be systematically explored and, ideally, resolved by interpretation. At these points in the treatment the therapist may need to interpret rapidly and in depth. Only if interpretation should fail, after repeated efforts to reduce the acting out, should the therapist instruct the patient to stop the behavior. The therapist then interprets the potential meaning of this behavior and explains why it was necessary to stop it. In other words, the therapist ends up interpreting the reasons that moved him or her away from technical neutrality, reinstating technical neutrality in the process. With a suicidal patient, the therapist might proceed as in the following example.

"Earlier, when you were cutting your wrists, I suggested some possible reasons as to what your underlying motivations might have been. At that time you refused to listen to me so I had to tell you that, should you continue cutting, I would have to stop the treatment. I did that because if you continued to harm yourself while in therapy, you would be doing something destructive not only to yourself but to the treatment. Now that you no longer cut yourself, we can return to the question of why you chose to do this to yourself."

There are several types of acting out. Ordinary acting out is reflected in behavior in or between sessions. The patient may start yelling, throwing something, coming late, leaving early, banging the door, instead of expressing the anger in words. Impulsive and self-destructive behaviors outside the sessions may include doing bodily harm to oneself, provoking aggression in others, or hurling oneself impulsively into chaotic, ill-thought-out "love" affairs. In contrast to these ordinary types of acting out, which are relatively easy to diagnose and treat, there are more subtle forms. One type is usually expressed outside the sessions and is reflected in split-off, long-term behavior patterns that often predate the beginning of treatment; this form is seen in "living out" rather than acting out patterns, although old pathological behavior patterns acquire a new significance as acting out of the transference. The therapist has to remain alert to what is going on in the patient's external life to diagnose this form of acting out, which is sometimes difficult because such acting out occurs subtly and gradually increases throughout time.

A borderline patient in his third year of treatment announced abruptly that he could no longer see his therapist because he had lost his scholarship due to failing grades, a fact that made it impossible for him to continue to pay the therapist. Only then did the therapist realize that for the past several months this patient had from time to time reported that he had failed to turn in assignments on time or do the required reading. As is frequently the case with such patients, he had consistently attributed (or explained away) these activities to some other force, such as to difficulty concentrating or to an overly demanding professor. Only in retrospect did the therapist recognize his lifelong pattern of destructiveness culminating in his need to destroy the treatment.

Another form of acting out is represented by very brief acting out in the sessions, sometimes taking a minute or less, in which the patient does something that leaves the therapist completely off guard and feeling paralyzed. The patient may suddenly say something that apparently changes the entire treatment situation. For example, the patient says, "Oh, I forgot to tell you that I've been pregnant for three months," and then goes on to talk about something else. There are two forms of acting out here: one, concealing something that has been going on for a long time outside the sessions; second, making a sudden statement that has a powerful effect on the session. Another example is the patient who suddenly tells the therapist, "I've decided I'm going to have a consultation with Dr. X, a major figure in the field of megavitamins, whose views about treatment are exactly opposite from yours." This form of acting out has a provocative quality, often creating considerable difficulty for the therapist, whose tasks are first to analyze silently the significance of the behavior and then to share his or her thinking with the patient. The process takes a lot of time: in the end, the patient's two-minute action requires the rest of the session to become elaborated fully! The technical approach for such acting out is to transform such "supercondensed" acting out into the therapist's narrative of what has been expressed in the therapeutic relationship.

"Your statement leaves me puzzled about several things that we now need to discuss. I assume that such an important decision was not made lightly by you but rather is the product of considerable thought on your part. If that is the case, I wonder what it means that this is the first time you mentioned it. If, on the other hand, this is not a carefully thought out plan, what does it mean that you would decide to do something this important in such a hasty fashion? There is the issue of what you are saying about me and the treatment, not only by seeking the consultation without prior discussion but also by the abrupt manner in which you present this information. I'm sure there are many additional issues as well, and somehow we need to look at them slowly and carefully, including understanding why you seek to attack our way of working together through this and other explosive announcements that you have made."

The counterpart of acting out is often somatization. As André Green (1986) has pointed out, intolerance of experiencing psychic conflict and pain may take the form of eliminating such conflicts through action (acting out), or by a symbolic transfer of the conflict into the realm of the physical and biological. The patient suddenly presents physical, clearly psychogenic symptoms. Most patients with ego weakness and severe character pathology, that is, those with borderline conditions, have a narrow range of tolerance for intrapsychic experience and quickly transform it into either acting out or somatization. What follows are some typical situations involving pervasive acting out.

The borderline patient's inclination toward alternate idealization and devaluation may give rise at some time to the experience of being in love with the therapist and to the expectation that the therapist will reciprocate such feelings—an experience that unconsciously devalues the therapist and the treatment. This may place the inexperienced therapist in an uncomfortable situation, eliciting anxiety, compassion, and perhaps even guilt over what has occurred. Insofar as the patient is able and willing to discuss feelings without acting on them, thus remaining within the framework of the initial treatment contract, the therapist will be able to continue the process of clarification, confrontation, and interpretation, while maintaining technical neutrality about the issue at hand.

Should the patient act out such feelings inappropriately within the session—for example, by attempting physical contact or by refusing to leave—the therapist should confront and interpret such action as the patient's effort to destroy the treatment by violating the agreed upon arrangements of the initial contract. As is typical of the splitting phenomenon in borderline patients, the aggressive component of the reaction is dissociated and the patient acts only on the subjective experience of love.

If the patient continues to violate the treatment contract, the therapist may have to take steps (for example, in a hospital complex, calling the security guards) to force the patient to leave, indicating to the patient that, for reasons they presently may not fully understand, such action is being forced on the therapist. Although the aggressive component of the patient's behavior cannot be interpreted while it is totally dissociated, the therapist ultimately must come back to it, exploring the motivation for the acting out as well as the therapist's motivation for taking action, an exploration that constitutes the therapist's return to technical neutrality. "While you were in the grip of the belief that I loved you and would make love to you after the hour ended, I had to have the guard take you out of the office. Now that you are able to leave the session on your own, it is important to understand your feelings about me and your belief that I would respond in a way that could only mean the end of the treatment."

Similar acting out within the session may take the form of refusing to speak—an example of the borderline patient's attempt to destroy time, concern, honesty, and cognitive understanding. As with all other attempts to destroy the treatment, the issue should be taken up when it occurs.

A wait-and-see attitude to the patient's refusal to speak is a dangerous therapeutic posture for several reasons: it supports the patient's omnipotent view of having the right to exercise unbridled aggression; it fosters the therapist's reaching a point where he or she can no longer contain angry frustration; it collaborates with the patient's devaluation of the therapist by suggesting that both of them sanction a do-nothing attitude. The therapist who consistently confronts the patient, however, demonstrates that he or she takes the time and works seriously. For example: "You sit here and stare at me, saying nothing. It is as if you are demanding that I accept that all you need to do is to show up. What do you think about what I am saying to you?"

In addition to confronting the patient's assault on the treatment process, it is also important to focus specifically on the patient's omnipotent attitude regarding time, as well as any contradictions in this attitude. "You missed the last session, and today you came fifteen minutes late. You act as if you have forever rather than that time is passing you by. Yet last week you mentioned that you were afraid to go to your class reunion because of your fear that you would see how others had left you behind."

Borderline patients are often heavily invested in sacrificing their own lives, while ignoring what they are doing to themselves. Interpretations must focus on how aggression is being expressed toward the self and toward the therapist, and how immediate reality is being ignored in the service of destructive ends. It helps greatly to point out to the patient that both therapist and patient are being victimized by an aggressive force, an "internal enemy," lodged in the patient's mind, and how the patient is tempted to collude with this internal enemy to avoid a justified fear of that threat from within.

The therapist can also be helpful under the conditions described by consistently interpreting the splitting between the patient's angry, demanding, and self-defeating attitudes in the transference and periods of calm, friendly, relaxed, and concerned behavior toward the therapist. There is a need to bring islands of potentially observing ego and of concern for the self together with the major area of the personality where unchecked aggression dominates.

Psychopharmacological Intervention

At present, three approaches to the psychopharmacology of borderline conditions predominate: (1) the avoidance of any medication during expressive psychotherapy, (2) the selection of a psychotropic medication to treat a specific target symptom or cluster of symptoms, or (3) the use of a medication to treat a psychiatric syndrome presumed to underlie the borderline pathology (such as depression, subclinical bipolar illness, attention deficit disorder). In addition to the application of psychopharmacology to the borderline disorder itself, medication also often has a role when the borderline disorder coexists with a specific psychiatric syndrome. For instance, many borderline patients also have major depression, so that pharmacotherapy of the major depression would be indicated. At the time of this writing, there is no consensus about the use of medications with borderline patients. In the treatment of borderline patients, the disadvantages of medication may not be counterbalanced by the benefits (Gunderson, 1986).*

*In the research study on which this book is based, we chose to limit the use of medication to situations where a concurrent major affective illness was present. A full discussion of the pharmacological approach to borderline patients is beyond the scope of this presentation.

If the patient has a major affective illness, full-fledged antidepressant medication is indicated. The same is true for cases with depression that do not fulfill criteria for major illness, but present neurovegetative symptoms of sufficient severity to interfere significantly with the patient's psychological functioning, such as slowed thought processes and verbal and emotional unavailability. For these patients, the pharmacological treatment should begin with tricyclic or tetracyclic antidepressants. After an adequate and unsuccessful trial, one should shift to monoamine oxidase (MAO) inhibitors, again using them for an adequate trial. Borderline patients may present concurrent symptoms of other psychiatric syndromes that require medication.

In all cases with depressive symptoms severe enough to warrant medication, those symptoms are expected to be significantly resolved by the antidepressant treatment. Obviously, the therapist must be assured of the patient's full and consistent responsibility in taking the medication, and avoid providing medication that could be used in suicide attempts. If after six months there is no significant change, all medication should be discontinued and the symptoms reevaluated. If a bona fide major depressive disorder persists after all pharmacological approaches have failed, that disorder should be treated with ECT. But if, as most frequently is the case, the symptoms really represent a chronic characterological depression, the treatment should continue without medication. Apart from the risks of side effects and abuse, long-term psychotropic medication tends to interfere with the experience and expression of affect; this, in turn, diminishes the therapist's ability to monitor affective responses within the transference. Medication has the effect of blurring the diagnosis of prolonged dominant primitive object relations, their affective quality, and their significance.

If a decision is made to use medication, it should be administered by a physician other than the therapist, whether or not the therapist is a physician. Otherwise, the giving of medication and the monitoring of reactions to it, with their intense transference-countertransference elements, are very difficult to disentangle from other transference implications.

The task of both therapist and psychopharmacologist in monitoring the response to medication is to differentiate changes in mood due to the transference from longer-term pharmacological effects. Thus, it becomes crucial to assess the patient's behavior over time rather than to be influenced unduly by statements about temporary changes in status.

Significant discrepancies often develop between the patient's subjective experiences and observable behavioral data. The patient may feel better and yet look worse to the therapist, or, more frequently, feel worse and look better to the therapist. The patient's subjective experience is, of course, the strongest indication of what is going on in the transference. It is easy for the therapist to attribute to the medication changes that are in fact due to the transference and to attribute to the transference what in reality are pharmacological effects.

One complication from the use of medication is that splitting may occur in which the patient relates to the medication as a "friend" under the patient's control. This occurs particularly with borderline patients who have strong narcissistic features in which issues of control are crucial. The patient may be highly motivated to use medication to deny the emotional importance of the therapist, and may try to show that their relationship is worthless. The opposite may also occur. Thus, it is important to continue unwaveringly a therapeutic approach of interpreting these issues. What may be very helpful in this regard is an open, ongoing discussion with the psychopharmacologist.

The psychopharmacologist must have total freedom to communicate openly with the therapist, and the patient should know that everything discussed with the psychopharmacologist will be referred back to the therapist. There can be no secrets between patient and psychopharmacologist that are kept from the therapist. Meanwhile, the therapist should communicate to the psychopharmacologist that which in his or her judgment is required for an optimally informed decision-making process regarding medication, and protects the patient's well-being and the treatment. A hypothetical exchange might go as follows.

Patient: Don't tell Dr. X, but I am not really taking his medications. I don't want him to feel hurt, but I don't take them. They are terrible.

Therapist: I think I need to share this with Dr. X.

Patient: Well, you can't say this, you are revealing confidential material.

Therapist: The main subject we need to explore now is, first, your efforts to corrupt my relationship with Dr. X, and, second,

your need to put me in a compromised position as a way
of testing our relationship.

The real theme in this example is the patient's displacement of the
transference. As this displacement is analyzed systematically, the patient realizes that he cannot change the subject matter (in this case,
the corruption of the relationship between the two therapists). The
therapist's unwavering refusal to change the subject until it is resolved
reflects, at a more general strategic level, the application of the principle and basic understanding of dealing with therapeutic emergencies.
As mentioned before, the highest priority is intervention for an emergency or danger affecting the patient's life, other people's lives, or the
treatment. The next highest priority is the emergency created by a
patient's dishonesty. When the therapist has touched dishonesty in the
patient's communications, everything else has to wait until that issue
is resolved; this may take months.

Sometimes the psychopharmacologist is perceived by the patient as
a vending machine, a perception with obvious transference implications. At other times, the psychopharmacologist is seen as the "real"
doctor, the one who understands, while the therapist is merely the
one who lives in fantasies and illusions. The therapist has to be prepared to deal with these and other transference implications, keeping
in mind how an ordinary person would react in order to differentiate
what is normal from what is pathological in the patient's responses to
the two therapists. A normal person would be equally respectful to
both, and would appreciate their communication and additional support. Often the patient is manipulating one while telling everything
to the other. It is important to have open communication to avoid
such complications.

The psychopharmacologist must spell out clearly to the patient why
medication is being introduced, what to expect from medication, and
under what conditions medication will be continued or discontinued.
The patient should be prepared for the possibility that certain symptoms will not be helped by medication.

The therapist who begins treatment with a patient who is taking
medication should take a careful history of previous treatment, attempting to differentiate pharmacological from placebo effects and to
identify the interplay of medication and transference. Medication

should be continued only if its use does not preclude a precise evalua-tion of the patient's present symptoms and if its use follows the appro-priate criteria for dynamic therapy.

A patient likely to misuse medication should not be given it. If the patient is depressed, for example, and is not complying with the precau-tions required for MAO inhibitors, the medication should be discon-tinued, and the question raised with the patient as to how the prefer-ence to be severely depressed can be understood. If a patient starts accumulating medication, prescriptions should be discontinued so that the temptation to commit suicide is not fostered. It is important to remember, however, that not all depressed patients are suicidal, nor are all suicidal patients depressed.

If the psychopharmacologist decides that the patient is not following instructions, then he or she and the therapist have to diagnose the situation and design a joint treatment strategy. Nothing can replace a well-conceived, individualized treatment strategy put into place by a knowledgeable psychopharmacologist and a knowledgeable therapist who respect and trust each other and each other's approach.

Environmental Intervention

Environmental intervention refers to the therapist's actions in in-fluencing the patient's external world. Hiring a companion would be one such example. Whenever environmental intervention for a border-line patient seems indicated, the therapist should ask whether it is really worthwhile, and whether he or she should carry it out alone (knowing that thereby the treatment will shift into a supportive modality) or an auxiliary therapist should be introduced. In general, if and when envi-ronmental intervention is required, it is by far preferable to introduce an auxiliary therapist and to establish a team approach.

Environmental intervention is used in dynamic therapy of borderline patients only under specific and limited circumstances—such as when the patient is failing severely in studies or work, or is drifting socially while giving clear indications in the sessions of a lack of adequate ego resources to evaluate or deal with reality. It is important to differentiate this latter situation from the manipulative smokescreens used by patients who try to confuse or deceive the therapist with vague and diffuse information about their life outside the sessions.

Environmental intervention may be warranted if the illness is being maintained by a chaotic family situation that makes it hard to define the patient's pathology. For example, a patient who overdoses has a mother who overdoses, as well, and a family in psychiatric treatment with bottles of various drugs all over the house, so that whoever gets angry desperately takes all the medication. Here, overdosing is a family mode of indicating unhappiness, while the designated patient is enmeshed in mutual pathological dependency and overinvolvement with the family. In such a case, an auxiliary therapist, preferably a psychiatric social worker, should work with the parents, the task being to render the patient's reality more manageable. The auxiliary therapist and the dynamic therapist maintain close collaboration throughout this work.

Environmental intervention may be effective with patients who are chronically dishonest. The antisocial features of such patients can be compensated for by direct environmental intervention. This is particularly true for patients who are dishonest not in the strict sense of lying to the therapist but in a kind of "innocent" suppression of information until the therapist asks about it. Basically, such patients refuse to assume responsibility for themselves and automatically and easily deposit the responsibility for their superego functions in the therapist. The auxiliary therapist in such cases should provide only minimal direct environmental intervention. If direct observation is required to the extent that an auxiliary therapist must spend all day with a patient and his or her family, a day hospital or full hospitalization may be indicated until the patient is able to observe daily experiences and discuss them fully with the therapist.

Short-term hospitalization is indicated when the patient has a severe symptomatic decompensation, has made a suicide attempt, engages in drug or alcohol abuse, exhibits a severe transference regression, or experiences emotional turmoil that threatens the patient's survival in the social system. Patients may require brief hospitalization when at risk of creating irreversible damage to their social situations, such as by losing a job or being expelled from school. Hospitalization may be indicated for a breakdown in the family support system; a psychotic regression that cannot be handled in the psychotherapeutic relationship; or a patient's being so distrustful, impulsive, indifferent, intoxicated, dishonest, unavailable, or aloof that one cannot make reliable judgments about suicide or other risks. Any of these developments activate the therapist's response to an emergency threat to the life of the treatment, the patient, or the therapist.

When the patient is hospitalized, the management of the treatment shifts to the hospital psychiatrist, while the therapist stays informed and remains prepared to continue the treatment after discharge. The therapist should normally not continue the treatment during brief hospitalizations because such an arrangement may foster regression: as the hospital surrounds a patient with a world of caretakers, the secondary gain of hospitalization may strongly militate against recovery unless carefully monitored.

Indications for long-term hospitalization (Kernberg, 1984; Koenigsberg, 1984) are limited to patients whose personality characteristics militate against outpatient therapy but who can benefit from dynamic therapy in a setting that enables them to tolerate it. These are patients with minimal motivation for change, minimal capacity for reasonable cooperation with the treatment, uncontrollable generalized impulsivity, minimal introspection in spite of normal intelligence, and a cultural and premorbid background that would ordinarily signal a capacity for symbolic thinking and communication.

Patients with severe secondary gain of illness that cannot be controlled while in their ordinary social environment, and patients who develop severe negative therapeutic reactions when an attempt is made at an intensive therapeutic relationship may also require long-term hospitalization. These indications include, for example, patients who cannot accept ordinary therapeutic structuring and cannot assume responsibility for controlling drug abuse, alcoholism, self-mutilating behavior, anorexia nervosa, or bulimia nervosa.

The indications for day hospital treatment are the same as for long-term inpatient treatment, except on a level of lesser severity. Long-term day hospital treatment must usually be accompanied by long-term treatment in the evenings, in a halfway house or similar controlled environment. In short, the combination of halfway house and day hospital may replace, for less severe cases, full hospitalization.

If the patient is to be hospitalized, a joint meeting of the therapist, the hospital psychiatrist, the patient, and the family is arranged to spell out the conditions of treatment and to clarify distortions in the communication within the family system. Such a joint meeting is the best way to reduce manipulativeness and the distortion of information. Spelling out the objectives of hospitalization, the system of monitoring, and follow-up plans can take place in such joint meetings.

Environmental interventions may tempt family members to engage in active manipulation of the auxiliary therapist, the hospital, or the day hospital. The family, for example, may threaten not to support the treatment unless the therapist does what the family wants. The therapist should be flexible and reasonable, but at the same time reject treatment arrangements that are not within the boundaries of what he or she thinks are warranted. It may become important to be very firm and to be ready to discontinue the treatment rather than compromise on the basic treatment structure.

A situation that evolves quite frequently is an approach from the family.

The patient's husband may call the therapist, saying, "I am very worried. You know I trust you; you are an excellent therapist, but my wife has been crying. She has been mute for the last three days and I am very worried that she may be seriously ill. I need to talk with you about this."

It is usually best for the therapist to say, "First of all, do I have your authorization to let your wife know that you called me?" If the husband says no, the therapist might say, "Unfortunately, we have to end this conversation because otherwise it would interfere with her treatment if I did not tell her about this call. Complete honesty in this regard is crucial for the treatment. So I'll respect your wishes, and only mention to her that you called, and that we agreed not to talk any further."

If the husband says, "You can mention my phone call to her, but I still want to talk with you," the therapist suggests that he first discuss this with his wife. The therapist may then talk with the patient, saying: "For me to meet with your husband is not something that I think would be helpful to you. But if your husband wants some help in his difficulties with you, perhaps a psychiatric social worker might help him."

Sometimes a relative's entering the treatment situation may justify recommending treatment for the relative rather than bringing an auxiliary therapist as an environmental intervention for the patient. If there are good reasons to think that the total system situation requires the therapist to be involved, collaboration with auxiliary therapists as described earlier is indicated. Although the combination of family therapy and individual psychotherapy with the same therapist has been used for a broad variety of cases, the expressive therapy for borderline cases contraindicates this approach.

Infringement upon the treatment may come from third party payers, as when insurance companies ask the therapist to fill out long-term review forms. The therapist should tell the patient about these forms, asking if the patient wants the therapist to proceed, and if the patient agrees, write out an honest and straightforward report, giving as much information as is necessary for an intelligent reviewer and as little as possible to maintain a maximum of confidentiality. Nothing should be sent out before the patient has a chance to see it: the patient should take a copy home, mull it over, discuss it with the therapist, and provide explicit authorization. It always creates problems to send reports because their technical language presents the patient in stark, cold ways that are different from the usual therapeutic exchange. Any traumatic effects must be explored and worked through.

There are times when the therapist should intervene directly in the environment. One has the option, under extreme circumstances, to provide direct supportive intervention through a third party. The therapist who cannot avoid getting involved with a family situation should stick with reality, analyze the meanings of the participation of everybody, and avoid becoming the advocate of either the patient or the family.

The therapist is at high risk when intervening outside the treatment hours. Such interventions, unfortunately, sometimes may end the treatment. As an example, a split may develop between the therapist and the psychopharmacologist. The therapist may have to tell the patient that there is a disagreement, and that the patient will have to choose which way to go. There is always the temptation to keep one's good relations with one's colleagues and to sacrifice a treatment situation in order to do so. But moral integrity requires a therapist to stand firm when a highly respected colleague does something or thinks in a way with which he or she cannot concur.

Should one ever have an extra session, or a session in a patient's house? Yes, if there are unusual circumstances, extreme situations, or emergencies. The therapist should be willing to provide additional hours if the patient is in a serious crisis, but should not reinforce those patients who are crisis prone.

Traumatic Intercurrent Events

Staying in role and maintaining technical neutrality are not incompatible with the need to deal humanely with a patient who has become ill, has experienced a serious accident, has become the victim of violence, or has suffered the death of a friend or family member. Such exigencies call not only for the appropriate application of principles of crisis intervention, but also for acknowledgment of the therapist's sympathy and concern.

In the presence of a crisis, the therapist must see that the necessary supportive network is mobilized, a task the patient often cannot do alone. It may be necessary to cancel or reschedule appointments. If the crisis is extended, the patient may miss too many appointments to make up, and then the question arises whether the patient should be charged for appointments missed due to illness, attending a funeral of a family member, or being hospitalized in the aftermath of an accident. There are differences of opinion among competent therapists regarding this issue; decisions about it become a matter of judgment and taste. The most important issue is that the therapist be consistent, both with each patient and in dealings with all of them: the application of similar ground rules for all patients will protect the therapist from countertransference acting out at times of crisis. In some cases, when a clear agreement has been made with a patient at the outset of therapy and when the cost of therapy is not a serious burden to the patient, it may be taken for granted that the patient will pay for missed appointments during crises. In many other cases the matter is not so simple. A patient struggling to pay for therapy who incurs heavy additional expenses as a result of an accident or an illness may present a clinical indication for waiving the agreement under these unforeseen circumstances. After the crisis is over, the meanings to the patient of the therapist's decision should be explored.

There may be periods in which the occurrence of numerous minor and major accidents strongly suggests a motivational factor in the incidents. Again, this should be examined after the immediate crisis has been resolved. When therapy has resulted in the patient's successfully controlling longstanding patterns of self-harm, accident proneness may supervene before the therapeutic work on the self–object relationship being enacted in the transference through self-mutilation has been consolidated. During such periods it may be helpful for the therapist to predict an increased vulnerability to injury and to explore its possible motives before an injury actually occurs. Such interventions may not prevent accidents, but they may enhance the patient's capacity for reflectiveness afterward.

CHAPTER 11

Severe Forms of
Resistance

Paranoid Regression in the Transference

Paranoid regression in the transference is most likely to occur in patients with borderline personality organization if they have marked paranoid, antisocial, or narcissistic features; it is less frequent in other types of borderline patients.

In a typical paranoid regression, the patient develops a special delusion in relation to the therapist while otherwise showing no evidence of psychosis. Three patients developed the following delusions:

- One patient thought that anonymous insulting telephone calls were going to him from the therapist's secretary.
- A second patient thought the therapist was being transformed into a bird hovering over her.
- A third patient was convinced that the therapist spat on the ground whenever he saw her on the street.

Although the content of the delusions may vary, what is characteristic of these regressions is their intensity, their relatively brief duration, and their focus upon the therapist as the source of the patient's distress.

These reactions may occur suddenly and unexpectedly; very often they run their course in a few sessions.

The relief experienced by a therapist upon the abrupt disappearance of the delusion, and the reproaches and criticisms associated with it, may lead him or her to avoid discussing the episode out of fear of reigniting the delusional state. Therapist and patient then remain unprepared for the next episode while the patient becomes aware of another method for controlling the therapist—a fact that may result in a feeling of triumph or of panic.

The therapist should be aware that a paranoid regression in the transference indicates the presence of deep and meaningful transferences that must be interpreted. Knowing this helps the therapist maintain equanimity during the episode, interpreting it and weaving it into the overall treatment rather than fostering its isolation or trying to bypass it.

Before it is possible to interpret the transference meaning of the delusion, one must clarify to what extent the patient can maintain reality testing. Once the patient and therapist have a common ground in reality, the work of interpretation can go on.

Three times within a year a patient accused the therapist of charging him for a session he had not attended. On the first such occasion the therapist thought he could have made a mistake and revised his bill. No further mention was made of the incident, but he took precautions to make sure his bills were accurate. Three months later the patient again made the accusation. This episode subsided spontaneously, and the therapist felt relieved since he did not have to confront the patient. He made no further mention of it, but six months later the patient, for the third time, accused the therapist of the same offense, saying, "You've done it twice before; you think you can get away with anything!" At that point, the therapist said that he believed the patient was convinced of what he was saying, but he himself was equally convinced that he had not overcharged. That left open only two possibilities: (1) he was lying to the patient; or (2) both of them were living in incompatible realities—in the patient's reality he was honest and right in what he was thinking; in the therapist's reality, he was honest and right in what he was thinking.

But these two realities couldn't fit together. The therapist went on to say that their predicament reproduced the situation in which a normal person and a madman were together in the same room—except that in this case, nobody could say who was normal and who was mad because there was no witness to the situation. Such a confrontation often comes as a shock to the patient. In this case the patient got enraged because, while he thought that the therapist was not lying, he thought that he was accusing him of being insane. As the therapist continued to insist that, because neither of them was lying, one of them must therefore be insane, the patient became depressed, remembering his previously reported experience of being sane as a child in the presence of his psychotic mother, who had insisted that she was right while the son had to struggle to hold onto his certainty of the reality of the situation. Thus, the paranoid regression had reproduced a significant pathogenic experience of childhood that became accessible to interpretation within the transference as a result of the therapist's keeping the delusional issue perfectly clear.

When the technique just described is carried out, patients typically get depressed, worried, and frightened. If they can tolerate their awareness of behaving "crazily," they are really tolerating a psychotic nucleus, and can continue working on what it means for patient and therapist to live in worlds that don't touch: what it does to human relations when it is impossible to establish contact; the distrust and fear evoked by the feeling that one is in contact with a monster; and the wish to humanize the relationship with the monster. In other words, the transference analysis occurs under the conditions of a psychotic transference, the gradual resolution of which may bring to light significant issues regarding the patient's past.

Working in this manner with patients with strong antisocial features, the therapist finds that when told, "Well, either we live in a world of incompatible reality or I'm lying," such patients readily assume that the therapist is lying, attributing their own psychopathy to the therapist. The therapist can then encourage the examination of what it means to be in treatment with somebody whom one wants to trust and who is instead lying, cheating, and exploiting the patient. The antisocial transference must thus be worked through; in the process, it is usually transformed into a paranoid transference and only then resolved. In general, the more antisocial the patient, the more unavoidable it is that the transference go through a period of severe paranoid regression.

To ignore these regressions fosters splitting, with the result that the regressions increase, and eventually the patient may interrupt the treatment. Issues from the past cannot be interpreted until the paranoid transference is resolved so that patient and therapist share the same view of present realities. Once the unconscious in the here-and-now has become conscious and reality testing regarding the therapy situation is restored, one can begin to make genetic reconstructions with helpful effect.

Thus, in the presence of a paranoid regression within the transference, the therapist must first diagnose the situation and then work with it to the exclusion of everything else. In making the diagnosis, the therapist must attempt to clarify the reality of the relationship as seen by the patient until a point is reached where the incompatible realities of patient and therapist are clearly delineated. In this process, the patient is likely to raise secondary defenses to prevent clarification, such as escaping into confusion ("Well, I'm so mixed up, I don't know what I am thinking anymore"), withdrawing, or becoming distressed in a way that diverts the therapist's attention from the paranoid situation. The patient may apologize, seeking reconciliation rather than exploration of the meaning of the regression. If these maneuvers are interpreted as efforts to avoid the painful recognition of the different worlds inhabited psychologically by patient and therapist, the regression can be resolved rather than being allowed to go underground.

Transference Psychosis

Transference psychosis differs from simple paranoid regression in the transference in that the psychosis expands outside the transference relationship to include secondary delusions and hallucinations. A transference psychosis clearly starts in the transference and then expands so as to affect other aspects of the patient's life. This expansion is more likely to occur if the transference issues remain closed to discussion in the sessions. It must be differentiated from an ordinary psychosis that arises independent of transferential issues. For example, a patient developed the idea that his therapist was having an affair with the patient's mother. He threatened to shoot the therapist and began carrying a gun with him at all times. The regression started with the analysis of oedipal conflicts in the transference and expanded into the patient's behavior outside the sessions.

If the paranoid regression expands in this way, it is important to begin as with a paranoid regression in the transference: to acknowledge the differences in perspective, and to tolerate them in the sense of not being frightened by psychotic thinking, while controlling the acting out of the delusional ideas: "Whatever you think and feel here is perfectly all right, but if these ideas affect you outside the sessions so that you can no longer maintain yourself within the bounds of conventional behavior, then we need to change the treatment."

The therapist has to prevent aggression toward himself or herself or third parties, and has to protect the patient. Transference psychosis can become indistinguishable from an ordinary psychosis; the test of the situation is the possibility of keeping it within the transference while resolving it. The therapist must be very direct and firm. If this does not work, the therapist must consider seeking consultation, prescribing medication, or insisting upon hospitalization for the patient. In expressive psychotherapy, such deviations from technical neutrality will require subsequent interpretation.

Brief Reactive Psychoses

Like transference psychoses, brief reactive psychoses extend beyond the therapeutic situation itself. They affect the patient's experience of others and may influence functioning outside of sessions. The therapist should clarify the extent of the reality distortions, the context in which they occur, the object relations involved, and any obvious precipitants. Any risk to the patient or others should be assessed.

Brief reactive psychoses often reflect extreme developments in the transference that have been isolated from discussion in the sessions, but may stem from sources outside the transference. One of the first tasks in managing a brief reactive psychosis is to reexamine the state of the transference and countertransference. A focus upon the transference in sessions may reduce the extent of the psychotic regression. As in the case of the transference psychosis, interpretation of projective identification and other primitive defenses often leads to an improvement in reality testing. When life events are precipitants of the brief reactive psychosis, the therapist should clarify the principal object relations activated and interpret the primitive defenses brought into play. Acting out should be blocked by limit setting. A brief hospitalization may be necessary when a psychotic episode places the patient in jeopardy or when the external precipitating events continue to maintain the psychotic regression.

Drug-Induced Psychosis

A variety of substances that influence bodily perceptions, mental state, or sensitivity to external stimuli may induce psychotic experiences in some borderline patients. In addition to substances of abuse such as marijuana and cocaine, prescription medications may be implicated. Drug-induced psychotic experiences include feelings of depersonalization and loss of reality, visual or auditory hallucinations, and paranoid delusions.

The management of drug-induced psychoses begins with the gathering of data about the patient's current drug ingestion. In addition to substances of abuse and prescription medications, over-the-counter preparations (especially those with anticholinergic effects) should be considered. The role of the drug in distorting the patient's reality testing should be explained. The therapist should clarify the effect of this information: Does the patient choose to discontinue the substance? The choice to continue should be explored, confronted, and interpreted. Some patients become involved in a vicious cycle in which the initial drug-induced psychotic experiences generate anxiety that the patient attempts to eradicate by self-medicating with the offending substance.

If interpretation is insufficient to resolve the behavior or if the patient is so disorganized by the psychotic experience as to be at risk or is unable to assimilate interpretive interventions, limit setting is necessary. Brief hospitalization may be indicated when the substance abuse cannot be controlled in the outpatient setting.

Erotic Transference

Sexual feelings for the therapist are common, as are aggressive ones. A therapist can expect strong sexual and tender feelings to be expressed at some point, by patients of the same sex and of the opposite sex. The psychotherapeutic situation is particularly tempting as a replica of the oedipal prohibition because in it strong sexual feelings are mobilized, while at the same time there exists a basic barrier against sexual involvement, as in the relation with the parents. The forbidden relationship can become tempting to the therapist as well as to the patient.

The therapist's unresolved oedipal and narcissistic problems may be activated by patients of either sex. If the therapist can tolerate homosexual feelings, they will emerge in consciousness in response to homosexual transference manifestations. By the same token, a therapist's heterosexual feelings are likely to be stirred within the transference. No matter what the relative age or sex of therapist and patient, their relationship replicates, in one form or another, the oedipal situation.

In normal love, the actual mutual relationship intensifies the tender and erotic feelings of the partners for one another, while if love is unrequited, it tends gradually to decrease and come to an end. On a deeper level, unrequited love activates the defenses against the oedipal situation and promotes the working through of mourning the unattainable object. As such, unrequited love has a growth potential—in both childhood and adult life.

Neurotic love, however, tends to increase when it is not reciprocated; and this is typically what happens to transference love. The lack of response intensifies it further and gives the opportunity for working through oedipal conflicts—for doing what was not possible before. Therefore, it is important for the therapist to tolerate the patient's loving feelings with the awareness that toleration will lead to working through of the frustration, the rage, the sense of humiliation, the fantasies of being rejected, the feelings of inferiority, and the insecurity regarding the other sex that everyone has.

Diagnosis of the erotic transference begins with the self-observation of the therapist, who must be willing to tolerate sexual feelings and fantasies about the patient without acting upon them, using them to understand what is going on between therapist and patient. In this process, the therapist must differentiate personal feelings of deprivation from responses to the manifestation of the transference. If a patient triggers intense erotic feelings in the therapist from the beginning, it may be wise to refer the patient to somebody else.

The sexual impulses of neurotic patients in the transference are usually repressed, and are rarely manifested in such a way as to evoke early erotic responses in the therapist. When, as a result of exploratory work, these sexual feelings become conscious but are strongly suppressed, sexual feelings may be activated in the countertransference.

By contrast, a therapist who has the capacity to tolerate chaotic countertransference feelings may remain entirely unmoved by the apparent direct seductiveness of a borderline patient. Such nonresponsiveness is an indication that something within the patient is complicating the direct erotic transference, perhaps erotization as a defense against aggression. In infantile personalities, intense erotic demands reflect the preoedipal longings for love, for preferred status, and for control over the therapist—all expressed in the language of sexuality but lacking an erotic impact upon the therapist. Antisocial personalities may consciously try to seduce the therapist for their own purposes. A patient may indeed seduce a naive therapist, with disastrous consequences.

Borderline patients with strongly masochistic needs may try to seduce the therapist in order to set up a situation in which they are mistreated. This may be subtle and difficult to handle, and can be very damaging to the treatment.

The goal of handling erotic transferences is to transform behavior into intrapsychic experience, as the following vignette illustrates.

A patient with schizoid personality and severe social inhibition came to the sessions disheveled, dressed in black, looking like a tragic, decompensated figure in a Greek play. She appeared totally unfeminine—except for her deep and revealing décolletage. She came regularly to sessions but remained silent, and the therapist found himself distracted by her breasts. Finally the therapist told the patient: "You are not saying a word. You come in disheveled and dressed in black in a way that would accentuate your being gender-less, as if one part of you is afraid of asserting your femininity in word or deed. Yet, in another part of you, you consistently come in with deeply cut dresses that reveal your breasts. Could it be that there is a message there: that you're split between one part that wants to be ignored as a woman and another part that has an intense wish to be seen, admired, and desired sexually as a woman: Could it be that conflict that prevents you from saying anything?" This intervention represented the beginning of the effort to move communication between patient and therapist into the verbal and out of the behavioral mode.

Many borderline patients make unremitting requests for love, in general, with few overt sexual components. The patient may behave in a way that is appropriate in social settings but totally inappropriate to the therapy. The therapist should keep in mind that his or her role is to treat rather than love the patient, that one has no moral obligation to love another more than comes naturally. Second, the therapist has to wonder why the patient has an inordinate need for love, and why of the therapist, of all people? What does the patient do with the opportunities for love that are available elsewhere? These questions alone may point to the patient's conflicts. In addition, behind the demand for love there is frequently a wish to maintain at any cost an idealized situation, which otherwise, it is feared, will veer into the opposite of intense rage, frustration, and disappointment. The patients who are saying, "Either you love me or I'll kill myself" illustrate most clearly that the real issue is the rage for not having an exclusive relation: they wish to punish the therapist by killing themselves.

The therapist must remain in role and be prepared for the patient's efforts to undermine that role by trying to create guilt with such approaches as: "You're treating me mechanically," "Can't you tell me where you are going?" "Can't I have a photograph of you while you are away?"

Narcissistic Resistances

The basic problem giving rise to narcissistic resistances is the incapacity to depend upon another person. Although patients who rely largely upon narcissistic defenses are, on the surface, very demanding, they cannot really feel that they are getting anything; because of their intense devaluation and hostility (defenses against deep-seated, unconscious envy), they cannot carry within themselves an internal image of the therapist as somebody helpful. They have to ask for more and more because, unconsciously, they have to destroy whatever they receive. What is missing for these patients is the normal relationship in which a person experiences a therapist as someone to be depended upon and trusted to be helpful.

The incapacity to depend upon another shows in many ways, beginning with a lack of trust in the therapist's genuine interest. Patients with strong narcissistic defenses have no sense of collaborative work: they analyze everything unilaterally, viewing the therapist as an admiring bystander. The therapist feels eliminated and is bored. Or the patient waits eagerly for interpretation, having nothing in mind because everything comes from the therapist—the patient is the eager bystander waiting to pick up all the pearls of wisdom. The therapist may feel very honored, like the greatest therapist in the world. It may then become clear at some point that this patient, who is so intensely eager, is not doing anything with what the therapist offers—just pocketing it and asking for more. These are indications of the inability to depend on another person.

Another typical manifestation of narcissistic resistances is subtle depreciation of the therapist by such statements as, "Oh, I knew it all along," or "You could have explained that to me months ago." The patient gets satisfaction from the sense that the therapist is not contributing anything the patient does not already possess. The therapist may also be perceived as a manipulative crook who must be defended against by learning his or her tricks; as totally indifferent; or as an enemy who has to be fought off—anything but as a partner in a mutually collaborative relationship. The depreciation may be deeply unconscious in borderline patients; the therapist perceives it and has to help them become aware that they are not listening; that they are curious about the therapist but not about themselves; that they are curious about themselves but totally ignoring the therapist; that they assume that the therapist is indifferent or dishonest or has only gimmicks that have to be acquired; or that they cannot let anything grow in themselves lest they would have to appreciate the therapist's help.

All of these narcissistic resistances may be hidden in an idealization in which the therapist is perceived as the greatest therapist in the world. This idealization enables patients to tolerate the humiliation of being in therapy. Behind this idealization, of course, is a projection of the patient's self-idealization. The narcissistic defense of omnipotent control is frequently expressed in insistence that the therapist's competence remain within an exact range: if less than brilliant, the therapist is depreciated; if the therapist appears to know something the patient doesn't, the patient feels humiliated. Thus, the therapist ends up feeling controlled.

Once one starts interpreting these defenses, the primitive transference of the ordinary borderline type usually emerges: intense rage against primitive parental images, particularly the relationship with a "bad" mother. One also finds intense and unconscious envy and defenses against envy.

Envy is a basic human emotion, typical for oral stages of development. Envy may appear as rage against the bad, frustrating object; but it is fundamentally rage against the good object who is perceived as teasingly withholding what he or she has to give. The negative therapeutic reactions characteristic of narcissistic personalities stem from their envy. For example, late in treatment, a patient said, "I heard what you said and I found what you said very helpful, but it pains me that you should be able to say something so helpful. Why can you do that? I don't think I could do that, and that pains me. And it ruins your helpfulness for me."

Even when envy of the giving therapist is the main issue, it may become complicated by envy of the other sex, a universal problem that is maximized with narcissistic patients. Other manifestations of envy include spoiling what comes from the therapist to ward off experiencing envy (Rosenfeld, 1987), forgetting good sessions, not enjoying what is received, and continually criticizing what the therapist has to offer. What is offered is either too much or too little, too soon or too late.

As therapy progresses, patients with a pathological grandiose self start to decompose it gradually into its component identifications.

What looks at first simply like arrogant superiority and devaluation become recognizable as identification with the behaviors of significant others of the past.

A therapist told a patient who was having difficulty with his college courses, "The part of you that hates the healthy part of you is trying to prevent you from learning anything from me, and this is the same problem that you have in learning in other areas. That is why, in spite of your high intelligence, you fail courses." The patient responded, "I don't fail in all courses. I get straight A's in everything except mathematics and Russian." It turned out that the patient's stepmother discouraged him from taking mathematics, because she herself was bad in mathematics. She also didn't want him to take Russian because the younger brother, the darling of both parents, had failed in Russian. The therapist had unwittingly touched very directly and concretely one aspect of the patient's pathological grandiose self: specific prohibitions of learning under conditions in which learning would put him in triumphant competition with sibling and stepmother.

In advanced stages of the treatment, narcissistic patients come to feel less empty; they become less demanding as they start feeling that the therapist is giving them something, because now they are able to accept it rather than having to reject it. They may tolerate envy better—suffering from it, but tolerating it. And they may start to become mournful and feel guilt over their ongoing aggression against the therapist. They may start being able to feel gratitude. Envy may be replaced by higher level feelings such as jealousy, which, unlike envy, reflects the capacity for a triangular relationship.

Negative Therapeutic Reactions

A negative therapeutic reaction is not simply a lack of improvement, but rather a worsening under conditions when the patient feels that the therapist has been helpful. Freud (1923) described the negative therapeutic reaction as a consequence of superego pressures, and of an unconscious sense of guilt militating against therapeutic improvement. As discussed earlier, negative therapeutic reactions may also occur out of unconscious envy of the therapist. A still more primitive type of negative therapeutic reaction, having to do with identification with a sadistic love object, involves a sense that one is loved only when attacked or mistreated. Here there is a condensation of pain and love so profound and intricately mixed that the patient cannot escape from it, and thus creates repetitive situations in which others are provoked to attack and reject. This enrages the patient but, at the same time, confers a sense of being alive. Patients with neurotic personality organization, and borderline patients in advanced stages of treatment, may present negative therapeutic reactions out of an unconscious sense of guilt. In contrast to ordinary sadomasochistic transferences, negative therapeutic reactions occur only after the patient has felt helped. Sadomasochistic interactions are chronic transferences in which patients consistently attack and depreciate the therapist, project that attitude onto the therapist, and experience the therapist as attacking and depreciating them. Rather than either giving up or counterattacking, the therapist must interpret consistently the patient's provocation without being controlled by it under the effects of projective identification.

Extended Silences

Extended silences, lasting from five minutes to practically the entire session, and continuing, from session to session over days, weeks, or even months, if not interpretively resolved, are not exclusively a problem of borderline patients. These patients, however, do represent the vast majority of the most severe and apparently intractable cases of this kind. Extended silences may emerge at any time, but are most common in the earliest part of the treatment.

If the patient does not respond to the therapist's invitation to discuss the causes and motives of the silence, the next approach is to ask what the patient is thinking, to attempt to stimulate the expression of whatever thought, feeling, fantasy, concern, wish, and particularly fear, the patient may have at that moment. Having done that over a period of several minutes, the therapist should now remain silent, observing the patient's reaction to his or her questions and comments. At this point, the therapist's attention to the multiple channels of communication in the therapeutic relationship becomes crucial. A patient in a room with a therapist cannot but communicate internal experience intensively, be it verbally, through behavior, or by means of the total object relationship that appears to have been activated at that point (which the therapist may be able to capture by combining direct observation of the patient's appearance and behavior with that of his or her countertransference reaction).

As soon as the therapist has a tentative hypothesis of the nature of the difficulty interfering with the patient's verbal communication, he or she should suggest what might be interfering with the capacity to follow the instructions that have been formulated, namely, to speak as freely as possible in the hour. For example, the therapist might observe that the patient looks more anxious after being encouraged to talk, indicating a struggle with an intense fear that blocks communication. Could it be that the patient is so afraid of the therapist's reaction to whatever might be expressed that talking about it seems too great a risk? Or could the patient be afraid to infringe upon some other fantasied prohibition or threat of punishment that might occur if inner experience were revealed?

The patient may respond to this interpretive comment by clarifying the situation and providing further clues to the nature of the resistance. Or the patient may remain silent; if so, the therapist should again let some time pass while exploring the communication that emerges in response to interpretive comments. For example, it may turn out that the patient now relaxes and no longer shows fear, but remains silent, with an apparent indifference or even a provocative way of looking at the therapist.

After some time, the therapist should again stimulate the patient to speak freely, and, perhaps, make use of this opportunity to repeat once more the initial instructions for the patient's and the therapist's tasks. In other words, in spite of the fact that the therapist may have gathered further knowledge, it is helpful to first stimulate the patient to talk freely, and then wait again for the patient's reaction to this renewed invitation to talk. If the patient maintains or even reinforces the behavior that emerged at the time of the therapist's previous interpretive comment, the therapist may, after a few minutes, formulate an interpretation about the patient's reactions to previous interpretive comments, and link this up with the potential reasons for the patient's earlier silence. For example, the therapist might say: "After I suggested that you were afraid to talk because of some danger that might come from me, you seemed to relax. Even more so, I wondered whether you were looking at me in a slightly defiant way, as if daring me to try to make you talk. When I invited you to say what was on your mind, this attitude of yours got even stronger, as if you experienced our relationship as a power struggle between us, with me trying to make you talk, and you trying to resist it. Could it be that this is the function of your silence at this point?"

Now the same process of (a) observing the patient's reaction to this interpretation, (b) waiting for some time while the therapist mentally interprets the new situation, (c) stimulating the patient to talk, (d) again remaining silent to examine the patient's reaction to this invitation, and, after some further time, (e) formulating a modified interpretation of the present situation, reflecting a renewed cycle of this approach to protracted silences.

For practical purposes, this approach, consistently and patiently maintained for as long as necessary, tends to resolve protracted silences within a few sessions. Very prolonged silences usually reveal profound sadomasochistic developments in the transference or severe paranoid regression that, once the patient has been able to verbalize fears and suspiciousness, should be handled as all other paranoid regressions in the transference.

BIBLIOGRAPHY

Abend, S., Porder, M., & Willick, M. (1983). Borderline patients; psychoanalytic perspectives. New York: International Universities Press.

Abraham, K. (1927). Notes on the psycho-analytical investigation and treatment of manic-depressive insanity and allied conditions. In *Selected papers on psycho-analysis* (p. 137). London: Hogarth Press.

Adler, G. (1975). *Borderline psychopathology and its treatment.* New York: Jason Aronson.

American Psychiatric Association. (1980). *Diagnostic and statistical manual of mental disorders* (3rd ed.). Washington, D.C.: Author.

American Psychiatric Association. (1987). *Diagnostic and statistical manual of mental disorders* (3rd ed., rev.). Washington, D.C.: Author.

Bibring, E. (1954). Psychoanalysis and the dynamic psychotherapies. *Journal of the American Psychoanalytic Association, 2,* 745–770.

Bion, W. R. (1967). Notes on memory and desire. *Psychoanalytic Forum, 2,* 272–273.

Carr, A. C., & Goldstein, E. G. (1981). Approaches to the diagnosis of borderline conditions by use of psychological tests. *Journal of Personality Assessment, 45,* 563–574.

Eissler, K. (1953). The effects of the structure of the ego on psychoanalytic technique. *Journal of the American Psychoanalytic Association, 1,* 104–143.

Fenichel, O. (1941). *Problems of psychoanalytic technique* (T. P. Wolfe, Trans.). New York: Psychoanalytic Quarterly.

Freud, A. (1936). *The ego and the mechanisms of defence.* New York: International Universities Press.

Freud, S. (1917). Mourning and melancholia. In *Standard edition of the complete psychological works of Sigmund Freud* (Vol. 14, pp. 237–260). London: Hogarth Press (1957).

Freud, S. (1923). The ego and the id. In *Standard edition of the complete psychological works of Sigmund Freud* (Vol. 19, pp. 3–66). London: Hogarth Press (1957).

Frosch, J. (1964). The psychotic character: Clinical psychiatric considerations. *Psychiatric Quarterly, 38,* 91–96.

Frosch, J. (1970). Psychoanalytic considerations of the psychotic character. *Journal of the American Psychoanalytic Association, 18,* 24–50.

Giovacchini, P. (1975). *Psychoanalysis of character disorders.* New York: Jason Aronson.

Giovacchini, P. (1979). The many sides of helplessness: The borderline patient. In J. LeBoit & A. Capponi (Eds.), *Advances in psychotherapy of the borderline patient* (pp. 227–267). New York: Jason Aronson.

Green, A. (1986). *On private madness.* London: Hogarth Press.

Greenson, R. (1954). The struggle against identification. *Journal of the American Psychoanalytic Association, 2,* 200–217.

Greenson, R. (1958). On screen defenses, screen hunger, and screen identity. *Journal of the American Psychoanalytic Association, 6,* 242–262.

Grinberg, L. (1979). Countertransference and projective identification. In L. Epstein & A. H. Feiner (Eds.), *Countertransference* (pp. 169–191). New York: Jason Aronson.

Gunderson, J., & Kolb, J. (1978). Discriminating features of borderline patients. *American Journal of Psychiatry, 135,* 792–796.

Gunderson, J., Kolb, J., & Austin, V. (1981). The diagnostic interview for borderlines (DIB). *American Journal of Psychiatry, 138,* 896–903.

Gunderson, J. G. (1986). Pharmacotherapy for patients with borderline personality disorder. *Archives of General Psychiatry, 43,* 698–700.

Horowitz, M. (1988). *Introduction to psychodynamics.* New York: Basic Books.

Jacobson, E. (1971). *Depression.* New York: International Universities Press.

Kernberg, O. (1975). *Borderline conditions and pathological narcissism.* New York: Jason Aronson.

Kernberg, O. (1980). *Internal world and external reality.* New York: Jason Aronson.

Kernberg, O. (1981). Structural interviewing. In M. H. Stone (Ed.), *The Psychiatric Clinics of North America* (Vol. 4). Philadelphia: Saunders.

Kernberg, O. (1984). *Severe personality disorders: Psychotherapeutic strategies.* New Haven: Yale University Press.

Kernberg, O. (1987). Projection and projective identification: Developmental and clinical aspects. *Journal of the American Psychoanalytic Association, 35,* 795–819.

Klein, M. (1948a). A contribution to the psychogenesis of manic-depressive states. In M. Klein (Ed.), *Contributions to psycho-analysis, 1921–1945* (p. 282). London: Hogarth Press.

Klein, M. (1948b). Mourning and its relation to manic-depressive states. In M. Klein (Ed.), *Contributions to psycho-analysis, 1921–1945* (p. 311). London: Hogarth Press.

Koenigsberg, H. W. (1984). Indications for hospitalization in the treatment of borderline patients. *Psychiatric Quarterly, 56,* 247–258.

Kohut, H. (1971). *The analysis of the self.* New York: International Universities Press.

Kohut, H. (1972). Thoughts on narcissism and narcissistic rage. In *Psychoanalytic study of the child* (Vol. 27, pp. 360–400). New York: Quadrangle Books.

Little, M. I. (1981). *Transference neurosis and transference psychosis.* New York: Jason Aronson.

Loranger, A. W. (1988) *Personality disorder examination (PDE).* Yonkers: D. V. Communications.

Mahler, M. (1972). Rapprochement subphase of the separation-individuation process. *Psychoanalytic Quarterly, 41,* 487–506.

Mahler, M. (1979). *Selected papers of Margaret S. Mahler.* New York: Jason Aronson.

Mahler, M., Pine, F., & Bergman, A. (1975). *The psychological birth of the human infant.* New York: Basic Books.

Masterson, J. F. (1972). *Treatment of the borderline adolescent: A developmental approach.* New York: Wiley-Interscience.

Masterson, J. F. (1976). *Psychotherapy of the borderline adult: A developmental approach.* New York: Brunner/Mazel.

Millon, T. (1981). *Disorders of personality: DSM-III, Axis II.* New York: Wiley.

Perry, J., & Klerman, G. (1980). Clinical features of the borderline personality disorder. *American Journal of Psychiatry, 137,* 165–173.

Racker, H. (1968). *Transference and countertransference.* New York: International Universitites Press.

Reich, W. (1945). *Character analysis: Principles and technique for psychoanalysts in practice and training* (D. Brunswick, Trans.). New York: Orgone Institute Press.

Rinsley, D. (1982). *Borderline psychopathology and other self disorders: A developmental and object-relations perspective.* New York: Jason Aronson.

Rosenfeld, H. (1987). *Impasse and interpretation: Therapeutic and anti-therapeutic factors in the psychoanalytic treatment of psychotic, borderline, and neurotic patients.* New York: Tavistock.

Singer, M. T. (1977). The borderline diagnosis and psychological tests: Review and research. In P. Harticollis (Ed.), *Borderline Personality Disorders* (pp. 193–213). New York: International Universities Press.

Ticho, E. A. (1972). Termination of psychoanalysis: Treatment goals, life goals. *Psychoanalytic Quarterly, 41,* 315–333.

Winnicott, D. (1958). *Collected papers: Through paediatrics to psycho-analysis.* New York: Basic Books.

INDEX